D0461200

The Reign of Charles V

THE REIGN OF CHARLES V

William Maltby

palgrave

First published 2002 by
PALGRAVE
Houndmills, Basingstoke, Hampshire RG21 6XS and
175 Fifth Avenue, New York, N.Y. 10010
Companies and representatives throughout the world

PALGRAVE is the new global academic imprint of
St. Martin's Press LLC Scholarly and Reference Division and
Palgrave Publishers Ltd (formerly Macmillan Press Ltd).

ISBN 0–333–67767–6 hardcover
ISBN 0–333–67768–4 paperback

This book is printed on paper suitable for recycling and
made from fully managed and sustained forest sources.

A catalogue record for this book is available
from the British Library.

Library of Congress Cataloging-in-Publication Data

Maltby, William S., 1940–
    The reign of Charles V / William S. Maltby.
       p.   cm.
    Includes bibliographical references and index.
    ISBN 0–333–67767–6
    1. Charles V, Holy Roman Emperor, 1500–1558.   2. Holy Roman
    Empire–History–Charles V, 1519–1556.   3. Holy Roman
    Empire–Kings and rulers–Biography.   I. Title.

DD180.5 .M25 2002
943'.031.092—dc21
[B]
                                                     2001058820

10   9   8   7   6   5   4   3   2   1
11   10   09   08   07   06   05   04   03   02

Typeset by Integra Software Services Pvt. Ltd., Pondicherry, India
www.integra-india.com

Printed in China

TABLE OF CONTENTS

For Nancy

MAPS

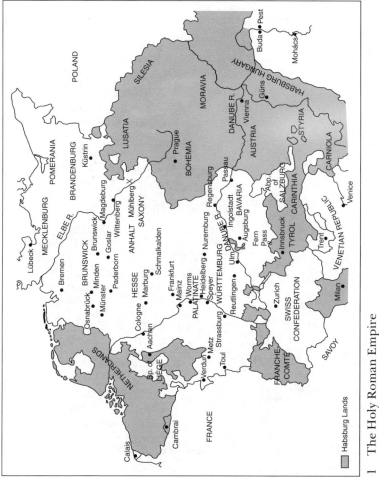

1 The Holy Roman Empire

2   The Netherlands at the Death of Charles V

3   Spain

4   Italy

INTRODUCTION

Few lives – and few eras in the history of the world – have been more filled with dramatic events or more important to the future development of both Europe and America than that of Charles V. His reign defies historical comparison. Charles lived from 1500 to 1558, an age that coincided with the later Renaissance, the Protestant Reformation, and the beginnings of Catholic reform. Though he ruled an Empire that stretched from Austria to Peru, it was an Empire with no heartland and few contiguous borders. Most of its component states and principalities were his by hereditary right, the product of good luck and the dynastic strategies of his grandfathers. His ancestors left him Austria, Spain, the Netherlands, and southern Italy, all of which had come under his direct rule by the end of his sixteenth year. More powers and responsibilities came to him when he was elected Holy Roman Emperor at the age of 19.

This vast accumulation of lands and offices threatened his neighbors and involved him in constant warfare with the French, the Ottoman Empire, and eventually with his nominal subjects, the German Protestant princes. Though often on the defensive, Charles continued to expand his realms. During the long and bitter struggle with France he added several provinces to the Netherlands, conquered Milan, and brought most of northern Italy under his indirect rule. In America his Spanish subjects subdued the great Empires of Mexico and Peru and laid the foundation of a Spanish empire that would survive until the nineteenth century. No ruler since Roman times held so many territories or disposed of such enormous wealth, yet even his vast powers could not solve the problems that lay closest to his heart. He did not stop the Protestant Reformation, which offended his deepest religious and political convictions, nor could he end the threat posed by the Ottoman Empire to Europe. Worn out at last by his responsibilities and weakened by deteriorating health, Charles amazed Europe by abdicating his many offices and retiring to a Spanish monastery.

This is not, however, a biography of Charles V, much less a detailed study of his reign. Either effort would be useful because there has been no attempt at a full-length biography of the Emperor in more than 25 years. The standard work remains the magisterial study first published by Karl Brandi in 1935, but Brandi emphasized Charles's activities in Germany at the expense of his other possessions and devoted more attention to the early years of the reign than to its darker, more ambiguous end. He also assumed more knowledge of the intricacies of German and Netherlandish history than modern readers are likely to possess. Since then, many scholars have contributed new information and valuable insights. The work of Manuel Fernández Alvarez (1975) partially corrected Brandi's neglect of Spain, and Martyn Rady (1988) has supplied an admirable brief summary of the reign together with a short selection of documents for the use of students. There has been nothing comparable to Wiesflecker's five-volume study of Charles's grandfather Maximilian I or to the three fine works on Charles's son Philip II by Peter Pierson, Geoffrey Parker, and Henry Kamen.

The reasons for this omission are understandable. The mass of documents produced in five languages over 58 years by Charles, his ministers, and his many governments is enormous. To master them fully would require a team of competent scholars whose findings would almost certainly have to be published in several volumes. Even if a bold, or heavily subsidized, publisher chose to support such a project, the effort might leave readers unsatisfied. If the purpose of biography is to illuminate the interplay of personality with events, Charles is a difficult subject. Throughout his life the Emperor cultivated the facade of dignified reserve and unfailing courtesy that he thought appropriate to his public role. A handful of anecdotes reveal something of his tastes and habits. Rare glimpses of the inner man appear in his vast correspondence, but for the most part the mask remains impenetrable. Even in the last years of his life when he struggled with debilitating illness and a 'melancholy' that would today be diagnosed as clinical depression, Charles did not drop his guard. He merely withdrew, locking himself in his apartment for days on end and communicating with no one. His *Memorias*, drafted on a trip up the Rhine in 1550, read like a state document.

When faced with an inscrutable subject, biographers sometimes resort to a 'life and times.' In this case such an approach would create even greater difficulties. Charles's reign comprised much of the later Renaissance, the Protestant Reformation, the conquests of Mexico and Peru, and bitter, event-filled struggles with France, the German princes, and the Ottoman

Empire. Europe and America experienced broad social, institutional, and economic changes, not a few of which were the immediate results of the Emperor's policies. To fully describe the context of these developments would require a library.

The perceptive reader will no doubt see in these reservations the whining of a detail-oriented academic, yet that same reader might with good reason be unwilling to suffer total immersion in the complexities of a distant age. This book is therefore intended for the non-specialist who wishes to know why we should remember the reign of Charles V. What happened in those years that changed the course of history and continues to influence the world today? I have tried to answer these questions as briefly as possible within the limits of our present knowledge and to provide an introduction to this complex subject for the student or general reader who wishes to place the reign in perspective. *The Reign of Charles V* will present much of what is known about the Emperor as a person, but its emphasis is on his policies and their consequences rather than on motives that are not always recoverable from the sources. In practical terms this means that the book devotes less space to the Emperor's youth, education, and the supposed impact of his physical and mental heredity than its predecessors. It compensates by paying greater attention to the institutional, economic, and intellectual development of his various realms.

Such a work cannot uncritically follow the conventions of narrative biography. If its purpose is to describe the impact of the reign on subsequent history, its structure must recognize, but cannot be based upon, the ruler's personal life. Ideally, it should also be brief. I have therefore rejected a purely chronological approach in favor of one that is at least partially topical, though many of the topics are covered in narrative form. The book's organization can best be described in a brief synopsis.

Chapter 1 describes the resources available to Charles at the beginning of his reign. It begins by narrating how he acquired the core of his Empire through inheritance and election and describes each of his realms with special emphasis on their political and economic situations. It then examines the personal attitudes Charles brought to his duties as a ruler. What were his views on politics and religion, and how, above all, did he understand his role as Holy Roman Emperor? The Emperor's habitual reticence and distrust of theorizing has ensured that answers to these questions have become the subject of controversy.

The second chapter describes the military and diplomatic struggles of the reign from Charles's election as Emperor to the early 1550s when he decided to abdicate. For clarity it is divided into three sections: the Wars with France, the Ottoman Threat, and what I have called the German Problem, a complex of issues that included the growing autonomy of the German princes and the coming of the Protestant Reformation. All three of these problems involved Charles in war. The decision to treat them separately was based on the fact that they differed in their origins and followed different historical trajectories; it does not imply that they were unrelated. Charles and his ministers rarely decided upon a policy in one area without considering its impact on the others. On more than one occasion his enemies put aside their differences and made common cause against him. The importance of these combinations is acknowledged throughout, but merging the three great conflicts of Charles's career into a single, rigidly chronological narrative has proved confusing in earlier studies of the reign. Compressing it into a far shorter book than those written by Charles's biographers would be worse.

Together, the wars with France, the Turks, and the German princes consumed most of Charles's life and had profound consequences in his own lands as well as on France and northern Italy. Like many rulers, Charles tended to see his position as basically defensive even when it was not, but the French wars, at least, added to his estates in the Netherlands and brought him effective control over northern Italy. The wars were in that sense a limited success, but they consumed far more wealth than could be received in current income. The system of imperial finance devised by the Emperor and his ministers to remedy this shortfall left a legacy of profound, if melancholy, importance to his heirs and their subjects. It is briefly described in Chapter 3 together with its effects on the development of European finance as a whole.

The most charitable interpretation of the Emperor's financial policy is that it was an aberration born of the need to pay for war. His overall administrative legacy was more positive. Though conscientious and deeply concerned with the everyday business of government, Charles V refused to impose cultural or administrative unity on his far-flung domains. He preferred instead to refine and expand existing arrangements, giving them the form they would retain until the end of the Habsburg dynasty and beyond. Chapter 4 deals separately with political and economic change in each of the major regions he governed directly: Spain, the American Kingdoms, the Netherlands, and Italy. Institutional change in the Holy Roman Empire, though equally important, is described in the appropriate narrative sections of Chapters 2 and 5 because it responded primarily to shifts in German politics rather than to the initiatives of Charles and his ministers.

The last years of the reign and the problem of how to divide the Emperor's vast inheritance have been given a chapter of their own. The book then concludes with 'The Reign of Charles V in History,' a brief essay that attempts to analyze the policies and decisions of the reign in the light of subsequent historical developments. That discussion is necessarily related to the place of Charles V in historiography, but no essay can do justice to the mass of literature on the reign or provide a useful guide to further reading. That is provided by an appendix, divided by subject, which serves both as an annotated bibliography and as a substitute for masses of footnotes. Because the book as a whole is intended for non-specialists, it reflects prevailing scholarly views. New interpretations are introduced primarily on issues that were not considered by the Emperor's traditional biographers. Because it seeks to guide its readers through the tangled narratives of a distant age, a chronology has been appended for their convenience together with a genealogical chart.

1

THE FORMATION OF AN EMPIRE

The child who would become the Emperor Charles V was born in the Prinsenhof at Ghent on 24 February, 1500. The building itself has long since been destroyed. The boy's parentage – if he survived to adulthood in that age of high infant mortality – guaranteed him an exalted position, but there was no way to predict that by the age of 21 he would rule much of the known world. That outcome was the result not merely of his own survival, but of a series of tragedies within his family. Genealogy makes poor reading, but the reign of Charles V cannot be understood without it. Everything he had or would become was his by heredity, and marital politics formed the basis of his rule.

Charles's mother was Juana, the third child of Isabella of Castile and Ferdinand of Aragon. Under ordinary circumstances Juana might have remained little more than a pawn in the game of dynastic alliances, but her brother Juan had died in 1497, followed by her older sister Isabella of Portugal in 1498. Isabella of Portugal had borne a son, but the boy's death in July, 1500, ten months after the birth of Charles, left Juana heiress to the thrones of Castile and Aragon. Charles's father was Philip of Habsburg (nicknamed 'the Handsome'). The son of the Emperor Maximilian and Mary of Burgundy, he ruled the Burgundian lands inherited from his mother and could one day expect to acquire his father's Austrian and German territories together with a presumptive claim to being elected Holy Roman Emperor. Both parents, however, were young: Philip was 22 and Juana 21. Charles of Austria, as their child was called, might have waited a lifetime before claiming his own inheritance.

The events that propelled him to the center of the world's stage came rapidly. Juana's mother, Isabella, died in 1504. In a move that casts doubt upon her presumed commitment to a united Spain, Isabella left Castile to Juana and Philip, who became King Philip I, rather than to her husband. Ferdinand was to be the kingdom's 'governor,' whatever that meant, but Philip understandably wanted no part of such an arrangement. He and a faction of Castilian nobles drove Ferdinand out of the country and forced him to protect his Aragonese kingdom by seeking an alliance with France. In 1505 the aging Ferdinand married Germaine de Foix, Louis XII's niece. Had his labored efforts to produce an heir been successful, Juana and Philip, and eventually Charles, might have been denied Aragon and its Italian possessions, but the marriage remained childless. Then on 25 September, 1506, Philip died unexpectedly at the age of 28, leaving his widow to rule Castile. It was thought that he had succumbed to the effects of playing tennis in the hot Spanish sun.

Juana, whose mental condition had begun to deteriorate even before her mother's death, now slipped into a state in which she neither could, nor would, govern. Some historians, echoing the sixteenth-century opponents of Habsburg rule in Spain, have tried to claim that Juana was not mad but the victim of a 'Flemish' plot to unseat her in favor of her son. There is no good reason to agree with them. Her documented behavior in public and in private supports a diagnosis of severe depression, perhaps complicated by schizophrenia. The Queen retired to the castle of Tordesillas where she remained until her death in 1555, only three years before her son. Charles, aged six at the time of her confinement, was now officially heir to Castile as well as to the Habsburg and Burgundian lands. With the death of his grandfather Ferdinand in 1516, he gained Aragon and its Italian possessions as well.

Throughout these troubles, Charles remained in his native Low Countries. He had an older sister Eleanor, born in 1498. Eleanor, after a brief marriage to the aging Manoel II of Portugal, would marry Francis I of France and play an important, though sporadic, role in the troubled diplomatic relations between her adopted country and the empire of her family. After Charles, Juana and Philip had four more children in rapid succession, Isabella (b. 1501), Ferdinand (b. 1503), Mary (b. 1505), and Catherine, born after her father's death in 1507. Eleanore, Isabella, and Mary grew up with Charles at Mechelen. Ferdinand and Catherine were raised in Spain where they had been born.

Charles's tutors, including the future Pope Adrian of Utrecht, instilled in him deep piety and a solid grounding in politics without managing to interest him in academic pursuits. As a young man Charles was physically unprepossessing – of medium size, pale, and with a jaw so large as to suggest deformity – but he preferred hunting, tournaments, and martial exercises to books. It was good training for a life that would be spent disproportionately on horseback and at war. His personality, too, appeared unimpressive, but his reticence may have reflected no more than an upbringing among the strangers whom he would one day rule. Reserved, courteous, and careful in his utterances to the point that early observers thought him a bit slow, Charles in time acquired regal dignity and a sure sense of command. He was not dull but careful, distrustful of abstractions, and conscientious to a fault. His clarity of thought and expression in political matters as well as his understanding of war are revealed in thousands of letters, many written in his own hand, but this vast correspondence affords few clues to his inner life. Reticence is useful in politics, but in this case it may also have masked a tendency toward mental depression that may have been inherited from his mother. It certainly increased with age. Even as a young man Charles was subject to periods of lassitude and withdrawal. In later years, over-come by illness and misfortune, he would suffer a severe, if temporary, mental breakdown.

The lands that Charles was destined to inherit comprised a vast patchwork of principalities that were neither geographically contiguous nor similar to one another in culture or traditions. The Burgundian lands, which he ruled after 1506 under the regency of his father's sister, Margaret of Austria, comprised the bulk of a larger estate built up by the Dukes of Burgundy in the fifteenth century. Burgundy itself, together with Picardy, parts of Artois, and the recently acquired Duchy of Lorraine, had reverted to Louis XI of France in 1477 when Charles the Bold, the last Duke of Burgundy, perished on the field at Nancy. What remained had been preserved by the hasty marriage of the Duke's daughter Mary to the Austrian Archduke who became Emperor Maximilian I. It included much of what is now Belgium and the Netherlands, but though these countries were perhaps the richest in Europe, they were far from united politically or economically. They were also vulner-able to attack from both France and the Empire.

For all their wealth and power, the Dukes of Burgundy had never become kings. Like them, young Charles held the provinces of the Netherlands as separate fiefs from other potentates. As a vassal of his grandfather, the Emperor Maximilian I, Charles was Duke of Brabant, Limburg, and Luxemburg; Count of Holland, Zeeland, Hainaut, and Namur. In 1515 he became Lord of Friesland, though several years would pass before the Frieslanders accepted his rule. Far to the south, the Franche Comté was also an imperial fief. The counties of Flanders and Artois he held from France, though the rights of the French King in these regions had long been ignored. Each province possessed its own administration, legal system, and representative body (the provincial estates), and jealously guarded the privileges it had won from past rulers. There were few commonalities of either language or culture. Some provinces spoke French, some Dutch, others both.

Charles also inherited a claim to the Duchy of Gelre (or Guelders) that would bring him – and his Netherlandish subjects – great trouble in the years to come. The heart of the Duchy was Gelderland, the area centered on Arnhem that controls the great river routes from Holland into Germany. Charles the Bold had acquired it years before in the course of a domestic squabble between members of its ruling dynasty. After his death, the losing side in the dispute reasserted its claims with the support of the Gelre Estates. With the accession of Charles of Egmond in 1492, Gelre emerged as a bitter enemy of the Habsburgs, launching repeated attacks against Charles's lands to the west and north. Its armies commanded by the fierce and capable Martin van Rossem and supported always by the King of France, Gelre and its mercenaries would remain a dagger pointed at the heart of Holland and Brabant until 1543.

Within the hereditary provinces were scores of cities whose own privileges made them virtually independent within their walls. The Netherlands was already among the most urbanized regions of the world. Perhaps 40 percent of a population of nearly three million lived in towns whose wealth came from cloth, manufactured articles, salt herring, and from a massive carrying trade that linked Germany and the Baltic with Britain, Iberia, and the Mediterranean. Antwerp, Ghent, and Bruges were among the largest and wealthiest cities in Europe. Like their smaller neighbors, they were governed by town councils and defended by militias. All of them held fast to their own laws and contended with one another, sometimes violently, over matters of trade and privilege. Even the Church, so often a unifying factor in other countries, was in the Netherlands weak and decentralized. The ecclesiastical organization of the Low Countries dated from an age long before the growth of major towns. Within the area of Burgundian rule, only Utrecht, Arras, and Tournai had bishops of their own. Other parts of the Netherlands fell under the jurisdiction of Liège, Cambrai, or Thérouanne, 'foreign' bishoprics whose affairs Charles could sometimes influence, but not fully control. The great population centers lacked bishops and, from Charles's point of view, effective ecclesiastical supervision.

Unity, such as it was, grew from a few common institutions that had developed largely under Philip the Good (1396–1467) and his son, Charles the Bold, though many of them had been weakened substantially after the latter's death. A Privy Council, staffed largely by members of the high nobility, deliberated policy and reviewed legal appeals directed specifically to the Prince. The Council of Finance, though in theory a subcommittee of the Privy Council, met separately and possessed its own building and cadre of bureaucrats. A central law court, the Great Council of Mechelen, had been established under Charles the Bold. It was disbanded after his death, and restored by Philip the Handsome in 1504. In theory, the Great Council heard appeals and adjudicated disputes between provinces, but several of the provinces, including Brabant, did not recognize its jurisdiction. It was most used as a court of first instance in cases involving ambassadors, court officials, foreign merchants, and others who did fall under the purview of provincial courts. The States-General, containing representatives from each of the provincial estates, acted as a central parliament with jurisdiction over tolls, taxes, currency, and the declaration of war. Its members, however, could vote only after presenting the issues in question to the estates of their own province and receiving firm instructions from them on how to proceed. Even then, no individual province was bound by the decision of the majority.

The Prince's revenues, as opposed to those levied by cities and provinces for their own use, came from a wide variety of traditional sources. They were rarely adequate, especially in time of war. Taxes could be levied only in the form of grants (*aides*, or in Dutch, *beden*) from the provincial estates or from the States-General and were not automatically renewable. 'Ordinary' *aides* in relatively modest amounts were granted with little controversy for several years at a time to cover the basic costs of government. The larger, 'extraordinary' levies needed to meet specific emergencies were another matter. The provincial estates and the States-General responded to requests for both types of revenue by presenting a list of demands and conditions that were drawn up into an *accord* and signed by the Prince before the vote. Redress, in other words, preceded supply. This gave representative bodies substantial leverage in dealing with their Prince, but created serious problems of governance. The estates recognized their reponsibilty to provide funds for the Prince, but regionalism and the tension between tax-paying commons and tax-exempt nobles tended to block requests not based on a dire and universally recognized emergency. If an *aide* were to be granted, one or more of the provinces might refuse to contribute if the money was intended to protect a distant neighbor, and even the provinces that supported a particular grant often wrote restrictive conditions into the *accord* that limited the way in which the money could be used. In any case, the non-renewable character of extraodinary *aides* made it difficult for the ruler either to borrow against the proceeds or to budget for much more than a year at a time, though this would change in the 1540s. Charles's Burgundian inheritance provided him with substantial revenues, especially on those occasions when France or Gelre attacked the Low Countries, but they were not at first predictable and never large enough to compensate for revenue shortfalls in other parts of the Empire.

In the midst of all this decentralization and local privilege, the titled aristocracy of the Netherlands emerged, paradoxically, as a force for unity. The Dukes of Burgundy had compensated for their lack of royal status by creating an elaborate Court with rituals based partly on the Mass and partly on the fantasies of chivalric romance. In so doing they gave visible form to the ideal of an aristocratic commonwealth whose institutional basis was the knightly Order of the Golden Fleece. The chapters of the Order, like the ceremonies of the Court, reinforced personal ties forged in endless tournaments, banquets, and other festivities. On occasion, they included sessions in which the members criticized each other's conduct. Charles, though Master of the Order, was sometimes rebuked in this way and responded humbly and graciously. Fortified by such bonds, the ruling dynasty and the great families that supported it came to form a cohesive society whose shared devotion to chivalric ideals was expressed in the most extravagant gestures and language. The nobles, of course, profited enormously from this association, amassing gifts, military commands, and offices. The ruler determined policy in a council staffed by the great nobles. Nobles served as the appointed *stadholders* or personal representatives of the Prince in the provinces and held a variety of offices even at the local level, where the wealth produced by their estates and their control of manorial courts reinforced their influence. Their younger sons tended to monopolize high office in the Church. For his part, the ruler gained from the Court the kind of loyalty that is based on shared values and the appearance of shared interests. It sometimes provided him with a measure of influence over representative bodies and in the countryside that he might not otherwise have been able to exert.

The obvious danger in this relationship was that it gave the nobles a proprietary claim on the dynasty and a powerful influence over the imaginations of its younger, more impressionable, members. The chief representative of aristocratic interests in Charles's youth was his Governor and Grand Chamberlain, Guillaume de Croy, Lord of Chièvres. The pro-French policies of Chièvres, traditionally Burgundian and typical of his class, brought him into frequent conflict with the Regent Margaret who continued to govern the Netherlands on behalf of her nephew. Margaret's vigorous assertion of Habsburg dynastic interests annoyed the French, but peace with France protected the wealth and property of the Burgundian nobility. Chièvres found it easy to manipulate the views of his young charge, and in 1515 engineered the ousting of Margaret and declared Charles's majority. That he justified his coup by claiming that the Regent had violated the statutes of the Golden Fleece tells us something about the power of aristocratic corporations; that the Emperor Maximilian accepted 140 000 florins as the price of his consent tells us even more about how the need for money could compromise dynastic policy. Forceful, intelligent, but narrowly Burgundian in construing Charles's interests, Chièvres remained the dominant force in his master's policies until death removed him in 1521.

The Burgundian legacy was therefore mixed. It provided Charles with a wealthy realm that was both difficult to govern and vulnerable to attack. It also left him with a fervent if unrealistic commitment to restoring the lost Duchy of Burgundy, and a mind steeped in chivalric and aristocratic ideals. Most of his biographers agree that the extravagant fantasies of the Burgundian court enmeshed him in a world that had little to do with the historical forces massing around him, and it is true that some of what Charles said and did, especially in his earlier years, appears anachronistic to modern eyes. If so, these anachronisms are a product of his Burgundian upbringing, but too much can be made of this. His contemporaries Francis I and Henry VIII used similar language to invoke the same ideals, and their policies are often as impenetrable to an analysis based on modern *realpolitik* as his own. The rulers of the day believed that honor was their most important possession and that it had to be protected at all costs. By honor they meant both personal dignity and the kind of reputation that could be demonstrated only in war against enemies of the faith or in support of their hereditary rights. Hereditary right was both sacred and eternal, the basis not only of the Prince's power, but of the entire social and political system in which he lived. No claim, however ancient, could be allowed to lapse. Charles held these beliefs without question, and expected his subjects to share them. 'Our honor and dignity,' he said, 'is your honor and dignity.'[1] For the most part the people of his varied realms agreed. To be the subject of a contemptible prince was both humiliating and dangerous. These ideas were rooted in the distant feudal past, but they retained their power until the end of the *ancien régime*.

The Spanish kingdoms that Charles would rule directly after 1517 bore no resemblance to the crowded Low Countries. Castile was a vast, mostly dry land of some six million inhabitants, the overwhelming majority of whom were peasants. True feudalism had never developed there, but freeholds were encumbered by obligations to nearby towns, the Church, the Crown, military orders, and above all, to a host of *señorios* or lordships. The nobles or *grandes* who dominated rural society had little in common with their Burgundian counterparts other than wealth and importance. Undomesticated by court life, their private armies had terrorized the countryside for much of the fifteenth century. Beginning with the Cortes of Toledo in 1480, Ferdinand and Isabella restored peace by reasserting royal authority and protecting the noble's economic interests while forcing them to tear down castles and disband their troops. The monarch's successful campaign against the Muslim kingdom of Granada absorbed the military energies of the *grandes* for more than a decade and brought them even greater wealth. In the long run this policy proved a bargain for the nobles who gained important privileges while reducing their expenses, but in some quarters resentment lingered. Most nobles continued to live away from a court that seemed to Burgundian eyes simple and even rustic.

Castilian government, however, was remarkably advanced. It was still based on the household model of the Middle Ages, but the reforms of Isabella and Ferdinand transformed it into what was arguably the most efficient and authoritarian state in Europe. The Crown was in theory absolute, and governed through the Royal Council, which had been expanded and reorganized in 1480. Staffed mostly by *letrados*, the lawyers who had already become the core of a trained bureaucracy, the Council not only advised the Crown but appointed officials and supervised their actions through a system of *residencias* (obligatory reviews of an official's conduct at the end of his term) and *visitas* (periodic investigations of their departments). The work of these councils was expedited by royal secretaries whose jobs depended wholly upon the favor of the Crown. Financial matters were controlled by the *contaduría mayor de hacienda*, which collected funds, and the *contaduría mayor de cuentas*, whose officals watched over their disbursement. A measure of corruption had crept into the system after the death of Isabella, but the institutional controls against it remained in place and were potentially far more effective than those available to other European administrations. The judicial system, too, had benefited from Isabella's reformist zeal. Unlike the Netherlands, Castile possessed a uniform legal code that in theory, and to a remarkable degree in practice, applied equally to all subjects of the Crown. After 1504 even the ecclesiastical courts were subordinated to their civil counterparts. The realm's chief appellate court, the *audiencia* of Vallodolid, had been expanded and reorganized, and in 1504, Isabella created a second *audiencia* at Granada to hear cases originating in the south.

In Charles's other realms, the Church retained much of its medieval independence. In both of the Spanish kingdoms, it was firmly under royal control. Long before the subjugation of the ecclesiastical courts Ferdinand and Isabella had gained the *de facto* right to appoint bishops and grant benefices through a long series of disputes and agreements with the papacy. Their control of ecclesiastical patronage helped them to reform the episcopacy and improve the quality of the secular clergy as a whole. They were assisted in their efforts by Francisco Jiménez de Cisneros, Archbishop of Toledo, Grand Inquisitor, and ultimately Regent of Castile. Himself a Franciscan and former confessor to the Queen, Cisneros used his vast ecclesiastical powers to reform many of the religious orders as well, beginning with his own Franciscans. Together, their efforts removed many of the grievances felt by lay people in other parts of Europe and greatly solidified the position of the Spanish Church. Should religious dissent emerge, it would be dealt with by the Spanish Inquisition, an institution unique because it was both national in scope and established under royal authority. Founded originally to deal with Jews whose conversion to Christianity was thought suspect, the Inquisition proved relatively popular in Castile, but had to be imposed upon the Aragonese kingdoms in the face of bitter protests. Though used only occasionally for political purposes, it provided the Crown with income from its confiscations while serving as a bulwark of religious unity.

The Castilian *cortes*, or parliament, had little power in comparison with representative bodies in the rest of Europe. Nobles, clergy, and commons attended, but the nobles, already tax-exempt and often co-opted by favors granted to them by the Crown, had begun to play an increasingly minor role in its deliberations. The ecclesiastical reforms of Ferdinand and Isabella, though they had improved the quality of the clergy, virtually neutralized them as an independent estate. That left the commons, but the only commoners represented in the Cortes were delegates from the 18 towns designated as 'royal.' Some of these cities enjoyed a thriving trade in wool or other commodities, but only a few compared in size or wealth to the towns of the Low Countries. The privileges they had retained from earlier times were severely compromised under Ferdinand and Isabella, whose personal representatives, the *corregidores*, enforced royal edicts and, above all, supervised the election of municipal officials. No one in other words could be elected to the Cortes without at least indirect royal approval. The Crown called and dismissed the Cortes at will, and even its consent in matters of taxation had become irrelevant except in the case of extraordinary levies or *servicios*. These grants, which became increasingly important during the reign of Charles V, had to be approved before the ruler would consider grievances or proposals for legislation. In Castile, supply preceeded redress, and the Cortes could not legislate on its own. The Crown was in theory absolute and free to accept or reject the suggestions of its subjects. Law could be made only by royal edict or *cédula*.

The Cortes was relatively weak in part because Castile was one of the few countries in Europe whose rulers had succeeded in imposing perpetual taxation. The *alcabala*, which dated in its earliest form from 1296, was in theory a levy of 10 percent on all transactions. It had long since become a capitation tax administered by the towns. Customs duties, the *servicio y montazgo* on the transit and pasturage of sheep, and the *cruzada*, or sale of indulgences granted by the Church during the war for Granada and maintained thereafter, had also become permanent and relatively predictable sources of revenue. Together these levies brought in more than 300 million *maravedís* in 1504. The Crown could budget for this and borrow against its receipts. Above all it did not have to approach the Cortes hat in hand for the ordinary expenses of government.

Castile, then, was a a large country with good natural defenses, a tractable government, and a Church that would prove impervious to the currents of reform that had begun to emerge beyond the Pyrenees. In 1512, Ferdinand had improved its security by annexing the tiny Pyreneean kingdom of Navarre and incorporating it into Charles's inheritance as a separate realm with its own institutions. After Columbus's discoveries beginning in 1492 Castile also claimed the Indies, a new world whose possibilities were barely discernible in 1517. Charles or his advisors must nevertheless have appreciated the importance of overseas discovery, for in 1518 he commissioned the Portuguese mariner Fernando Magellan to seek the Moluccas by sailing west. The expedition reached the Philippines and claimed the Moluccas before Magellan's death in a fight with natives on the island of Mactán. A remnant of his men under Sebastian del Cano then completed the first circumnavigation of the globe under terrible conditions before reaching Seville, where they were personally received by Charles in 1522.

Charles sold the Moluccas to Portugal in 1529, thereby ensuring Portuguese supremacy in the east for years to come. The Spanish claim to the Philippines was not revived until 1565. The Americas, however, would one day pay huge dividends to Spain, though Charles at first did little to exploit the discoveries himself. At the beginning of his reign he probably felt that the Spanish army was a more useful acquisition. Through the long, bitter war for Granada and the even longer struggles in Italy, Ferdinand of Aragon had built up the finest army in Europe: a force of tough, Castilian peasants, well trained by professional officers drawn mostly from the lesser nobility. Under the 'Great Captain,' Gonzalo de Córdoba, they had mastered the coordination of pikes with shot and developed the tactics that would dominate battlefields for more than a century. The army's quality had declined since its defeat by the French and Swiss at the Battle of Marignano in 1515. The failure cost Ferdinand Milan, but no one doubted that the army itself could be revived. Its cadres remained intact and economic conditions in the mountains and bleak tablelands of Castile ensured that there would always be an abundance of recruits. With permanent taxation and a military that would become the elite core of the imperial armies, Castile was truly a prize worth having, yet securing it proved unexpectedly difficult.

Aragon, the smaller of the two kingdoms with a population of perhaps a million, was divided into three parts: Aragon proper, a harsh, sparsely populated region of large estates; Catalonia, centered on the once-prosperous city of Barcelona; and Valencia, whose urban core was surrounded by a large population of Moorish agriculturalists. Aragon was Castilian in language and culture, though fiercely resistant to Castilian institutions. Catalans and Valencians had their own languages. All three had protected their privileges (*fueros*) during the long reign of Ferdinand, and their representative bodies had never granted a perpetual tax, nor had they given up the right to demand a redress of grievances before supplying money. Charles could therefore expect little in the way of increased revenues from his Aragonese subjects.

The remainder of the Aragonese patrimony included the Italian kingdoms of Sicily, Sardinia, and Naples. Sicily had been for all practical purposes Aragonese since 1282; Sardinia since the fourteenth century.

Alfonso V of Aragon had conquered Naples in 1442. In the course of defending the kingdoms against French claims, Ferdinand had acquired them from a cadet branch of his own family and incorporated them into his domains by 1504. Each state was governed by a viceroy and had a *parlamentum* that voted on revenue measures, but their representative bodies were very different in character. Of the three, the Sicilian parliament was in theory the most powerful. It had three *bracci*, or estates: ecclesiastical, military (the titled nobility), and domainal, which represented a variety of corporations including cities and the university. As in the Netherlands, redress preceded supply, but in fact the Sicilians would remain among Charles's most compliant subjects. Every three years they provided an 'ordinary' grant equivalent to 100 000 florins which rose to 175 000 later in the reign. Extraordinary grants were made in a total of ten years beginning in 1532. Sicilian complacency was due in part to the political skill of Charles's viceroys, and in part to the fact that the kingdom needed constant protection from Muslim raiders based on the nearby ports of North Africa. Sicily, however, was relatively poor, and its revenues proved barely sufficient for its own needs. Much the same could be said of Sardinia, though its institutions were far less developed than those of Sicily and its *parlementum* was controlled entirely by the local nobility.

Naples, though richer in absolute terms than Charles's other Italian kingdoms, proved the most difficult to govern. A faction-ridden nobility, often allied with bandit gangs, dominated a weak *parlementum* in which supply preceded redress. The clergy were not represented. The city of Naples, then as now a huge complex with more than its fair share of the urban poor, had its own representative institutions or *seggi*. The kingdom had rebelled against an unpopular viceroy in 1516, but Charles's appointments, especially the able Don Pedro de Toledo who ruled from 1532–53, maintained a degree of order by playing one faction of nobles against the other. The vigorous and often bloody campaigns of the viceroys against the *banditi* proved less successful. In the early years of the reign, the weakness of Neapolitan parliamentary institutions helped to ensure a much-needed flow of revenue. Later, the constant demands of the government caused such hardship that even the viceroys were forced to protest. Naples, however, like the other Italian kingdoms, proved generally loyal and supportive of Charles. Together, they gave him an essential base in Italy for his wars against France while broadening his exposure to conflict with the Muslim states of North Africa and their allies the Turks.

Charles sailed from the Netherlands to claim his Spanish inheritance in 1517, accompanied by Chièvres and a contingent of Burgundian courtiers who hoped to profit from their master's good fortune. From the moment his fleet landed in northern Castile the new ruler was met with suspicion that rapidly hardened into hostility. Charles did not yet speak Spanish and his 'Flemish' entourage quickly made themselves offensive to the Castilians, but many of the problems he faced arose from a delayed reaction to the policies of Ferdinand and Isabella or to the partial breakdown of government during the disputes between Ferdinand and Philip the Handsome. There was much accumulated resentment over the actions of royal judges and tax collectors and widespread hostility to a scheme recently put forth by Cardinal Cisneros to establish a permanent body of troops called the *gentes de ordenanza*. The cities, in particular, had long been outraged by the appointment of unqualified and often corrupt *corregidores* and by the widespread failure to conduct *residencias*. Tensions increased under the regency of Cisneros, a man whose autocratic disposition did not improve with age. When he died shortly after Charles's arrival, even the clergy found the courage to protest the loss of their immunities so many years before.

Chièvres mismanaged this dangerous situation from the start. With an indifference to Spanish sensibilities that only greed could justify, he encouraged the new King to enrich his Burgundian entourage at Spanish expense. Chièvres had himself named *contador mayor*, the most important financial officer in the realm; then sold the office to the Spanish Duke of Béjar for ready cash. Chièvres's 18-year-old nephew was named Archbishop of Toledo. Even the first meeting of the Castilian Cortes convened under the presidency of a foreigner, the Grand Chancellor Jean de Sauvage. The members protested the presence of foreigners in their midst, but after Charles swore to uphold the laws of Castile they voted him a three-year subsidy of 600 000 ducats. The more independent Cortes of Aragon required nine months to recognize Charles, and then only as joint ruler with his mother. That of Valencia refused to recognize him at all unless he visited the kingdom. The Catalan *corts* proved equally difficult. Charles was still negotiating with them when he was elected Holy Roman Emperor on 28 June, 1519. For the Castilian towns, their King's election as Emperor was the last straw. Charles now planned to leave for Germany in pursuit of goals that could only harm their interests. Castilian blood and treasure would surely be sucked into the morass of German politics. Worse yet, he planned to appoint another 'Fleming,' his old tutor Adrian of Utrecht, as their regent. When

Charles asked the Cortes of Castile for another subsidy in March, 1520, they refused. This was unconstitutional and unprecedented. The subsidy finally passed with 10 of the 18 royal towns abstaining, but it was never collected. When Charles left for Germany in May, 1520, several cities were in open rebellion. The revolt of the *comuneros* had begun.

The election of the young Prince as Emperor Charles V was no surprise, but the result of long and careful planning. In 1356 the Golden Bull formalized existing practice by decreeing that the Holy Roman Emperor should be chosen by a majority of seven Electors: the Margrave of Brandenburg, the Duke of Saxony, the King of Bohemia, the Count Palatine of the Rhine, and the Archbishops of Mainz, Trier, and Cologne. Ruling emperors, however, sometimes attempted to secure the election of a successor during their lifetime by having the Electors name him King of the Romans, the title held by imperial nominees prior to their coronation by the pope. Charles's grandfather, the Emperor Maximilian I, had every intention of doing just that, but died in January, 1519, before his plans for his grandson's succession were complete. This opened the field to others, including Francis I of France, Henry VIII of England, and Frederick the Wise of Saxony, a shrewd politician who refused to mention his own candidacy but allowed others to speak for him. The Elector's precise intentions are unclear to this day. Unlike Francis and Henry, Charles was a prince of the Empire by virtue of his holdings in the Low Countries. Maximilian's death brought him the Habsburg possessions in central Europe as well. These included Austria, Styria, Carinthia, and Tyrol as well as the landgrave of Alsace and several counties in Swabia and the Breisgau. In his will of 31 December, 1518, Maximilian bequeathed these lands jointly to Charles and his brother Ferdinand, but designated Charles as the 'senior.' For the moment, at least, Charles elected to assume that this gave him full possession. His propagandists therefore touted him as the German candidate, though he could not speak German and had never set foot in Germany. The value of such appeals was questionable. In the end Charles secured his election through massive bribery backed by the threat of force.

The cost of the campaign exceeded 835 000 florins. The electors received 332 000 of this as outright bribes, much of it in the form of bills payable only in the event of Charles's election. Neither Francis nor Henry could match this effort. Henry's relative poverty meant that he was not really in the running. France was the richest kingdom in Europe, but the credit of its king was poor and Francis had to pay cash to the electors in advance. Thanks to the promise of permanent revenues from Castile and the Tyrol, Charles could draw on the goodwill of German and Italian bankers. The Fuggers of Augsburg, then Europe's greatest bankers, alone contributed 542 000 florins or 65 percent of the total. The Fugger loans marked the beginning of a long-term relationship that would become one of the cornerstones of Charles's power.

   Financially, the electors had everything to gain by taking the money from Francis and then voting for Charles, but they had to consider the military consequences of such an act. At the beginning of 1519, Charles had few military assets in the Empire with which to counter the French or to intimidate the Germans. This changed when Duke Ulrich of Württemberg's attack on the neighboring city of Reutlingen mobilized the army of the Swabian League, a confederation of southwest German towns and princes. The Swabians quickly occupied the Duke's territories, and then, encouraged by payments from Charles's agents, remained in the field as supporters of the Habsburg cause. The Swiss, too, joined the Habsburg cause in return for 30 000 florins and because they, like the Swabians, saw Ulrich as a tool of the French. Another 40 000 florins bought the services of the great military contractor Franz von Sickingen and his *Landsknechte*. The military situation was reversed. The electors could now indulge their greed without fear of reprisal from either the French or from the German friends of Frederick the Wise. Pope Leo X, believing that the French cause was now lost and irritated by Francis's ill-timed decision to assert his claim to the Duchy of Urbino in the Papal States, withdrew his opposition to Charles's candidacy. Frederick of Saxony declined a last-minute effort to recruit him as an anti-Habsburg alternative, and Charles, after signing an agreement to preserve imperial institutions, was elected Emperor by a unanimous vote on 28 June, 1519.[2]

   The imperial office brought Charles great prestige and even greater problems. The Holy Roman Empire was, as it had been for centuries, an unstable amalgam of more than 200 princely states and free cities. Some of the principalities were as large and populous as the kingdoms of Scotland or Sweden; others were very small. There was also a host of tiny fiefs held directly from the Emperor by a class of smallholders known as Imperial Knights. Instability arose not only from rivalry among the princely dynasties, but from the use of partible inheritance which caused the endless division and re-formation of principalities and encouraged rulers to think of their states as personal property. The late-medieval Empire suffered from widespread social and economic tensions as well. The demographic catastrophe created by the Black Death had diminished the revenues of all landholders by reducing rents and property values while increasing wages. Lesser nobles and the Imperial Knights, whose fiefs were often no more than small farms, could do little about this. In the course of the fifteenth century they sank into poverty, or, if they possessed the necessary skills, became mercenaries. Some descended to outright banditry. The problem for the larger principalities, both lay and ecclesiastical, was that the cost of war increased dramatically as their revenues declined. Survival depended upon measures which, though partially effective, tended to heighten social instability. Almost without exception they squeezed the peasants by reintroducing obsolete labor services, restricting inheritance, strengthening the forest laws, and devising new taxes. The peasants could do little to defend themselves. Peasants were excluded from all but a few of the *Landstände* or representative bodies within the German states. Protests, if they dared to make them, were heard by manorial courts controlled by their oppressors. Their frustration expressed itself in localized peasant revolts that became common in the fifteenth century, some of them under the symbol of the *Bundschuh* or peasant boot. These rebellions would culminate in the Great Peasant's War of 1524–26, a cataclysm that engulfed much of central and southern Germany.

Efforts to increase revenue brought the princes into conflict with their *Landstände* as well. Representatives, whatever their estate, disliked the tendency of rulers to confuse public with private expenditures and valiantly resisted taxes. In some cases the princes put pressure on their proprietary towns by trying to reduce privileges, but this seems to have worked well only in Brandenburg. By 1519 the princely states were still hungry for revenues and jealous of their independence. They were, however, richer and better organized internally than they had been a century before. Most of them had at last decided to preserve their territorial integrity by adopting primogeniture, though Saxony was still divided into an Electoral and a Ducal state, each ruled by a different branch of the Wettin family, and there were still two Dukes of Bavaria, though Bavaria itself would be reunited in 1521 under their joint rulership. Whatever their dynastic arrangements, all of the princes had at least rudimentary bureaucracies and governed through councils that were gradually becoming permanent. The larger of the states already resembled the monarchies of western Europe in everything but the possession of a royal title.

An emperor's ability to govern depended almost entirely upon his own hereditary resources and force of personality. By tradition he ruled only with the consent of the Imperial Diet, a representative assembly whose sheer size and diversity of interests made agreement almost impossible. The Diet was divided into three 'colleges': the Electors, the princes, including the bishops and prince-abbots, and the towns, whose members represented the imperial cities. The Emperor convened the Diet with the consent of the Electors, and presented a list of propositions that were debated separately by each college. When the Electors, under the presidency of the Archbishop of Mainz, reached agreement, they consulted the princes. Then the Electors and princes might or might not consult the towns. Until 1648, the towns could not cast a deciding vote.

Aside from the Diet and an imperial chancellery that registered its decrees, imperial institutions were few. Charles's grandfather and predecessor, Maximilian I, had tried to remedy the situation by creating an imperial court, an expanded administration, and a system of uniform taxation. A visionary who wanted to reform the Empire with himself as ruler of a united Christendom, he even toyed at one point with the idea of becoming both Pope and Emperor. The princes, too, wanted reform, but they wanted it on different terms. On balance, the princes won. In the 1490s Maximilian gained approval for an imperial court (the *Reichskammergericht*) that could resolve disputes between states, but the majority of its judges were to be named by the Imperial Diet rather than the Emperor. The Common Penny, a universal tax, was to be collected by the Diet as well. Many states and cities refused to pay it, and the Swiss used it as an excuse to leave the Empire in 1499. The system of imperial circles (*Kreise*), intended by Maximilian to provide a measure of regional control by dividing the Empire into administrative districts, fell under princely influence as well. In 1500 the Diet even established an Imperial Governing Council to check the Emperor's dominance in the conduct of foreign policy, but Maximilian, like his successors, found it easy to sidestep its influence. The Council was dissolved in 1502, restored in 1521, and abolished by Charles for the last time in 1530.

In the light of these problems it might seem that 'imperial rule' was an oxymoron, but Charles knew that this was not entirely the case. Bitter and often ancient rivalries made it difficult for the princes to present a united front. Moreover, as his experience with the Swabian League had shown, Charles had potential allies in the imperial cities. Few German cities were as large as their counterparts in the Netherlands, but they had achieved greater independence. The age of imperial devolution after the fall of the imperial Hohenstaufen dynasty in the thirteenth century left them with many of the privileges characteristic of city states and a deep suspicion of the princes. Imperial institutions, too, proved more open to manipulation than the princes had supposed. Tact and compromise could produce favorable agreements in the Imperial Diet. Because the princes chose not to attend the Governing Council in person, the Emperor could sometimes use it as a vehicle for communicating his policies as well. Even the *Reichskammergericht* would develop into a useful weapon against the Protestants after the outbreak of the Reformation.[3]

Charles would need all of this and more if he were to maintain some measure of influence over events. He appears to have had few illusions about changing the constitutional basis of imperial power, nor did he at any time expect to create something as far-fetched as a German monarchy based on the French or Spanish model. Even the *Constitutio criminalis Carolina*, the uniform criminal code adopted by the Empire in 1532, owed nothing to his influence, though it bears his name. At best, Charles hoped to preserve and, if possible, augment the historic powers of his office while ensuring that it would remain within the family after his death. But even these relatively modest goals would be threatened by the outbreak of a religious dispute that had reached dangerous proportions by the time of his election.

The Reformation was the most important event of Charles's reign, and his failure to stem it remains the measure by which he has most frequently been judged by historians. No one doubts that the movement begun by Martin Luther shattered the religious unity of the west, or that, on a less apocalyptic level, it influenced the Emperor's policies in nearly every area. At the very least, it was never far from his mind. For German historians of another age, regardless of their confessional preferences, the Reformation delayed the unification of Germany for centuries. This view assumes a measure of historical inevitability that was not evident in the sixteenth century, but if there were other compelling reasons for German disunity, the Reformation added to them and provided new sources of conflict. Above all, religious reform placed powerful new weapons in the hands of princes and cities alike that made it easier for them to resist imperial pretensions.

In 1517 Martin Luther, the Augustinian monk and Professor of New Testament at the University of Wittenberg, launched his protest against the sale of indulgences by the papacy. When his views on this subject were condemned, his thought moved beyond the original issue to a generalized attack on papal authority and, in time, to a condemnation of the medieval Church's views on justification and the sacraments. Reformist enthusiasm spread through Germany, fanned by Luther's eloquence and by the underlying anticlericalism of many Germans who had long resented clerical privileges and exactions. By the time Charles was ready to convene his first Imperial Diet at Worms in January, 1521, the Church had excommunicated Luther after rejecting 41 of his propositions. Luther's followers responded by publically burning the bull of excommunication, but neither the princes nor the towns seemed willing to confront the religious turmoil head-on. The spark ignited in 1517 had become a conflagration.

Luther's celebrated appearance before the Diet of Worms was both irregular and peripheral to the Diet's basic agenda. In autumn, 1520, the papal envoy Aleander asked that Luther be outlawed. Charles, devout and orthodox to the core of his being, would have agreed had not Luther's own prince, Frederick the Wise, protested. Under the agreement signed by Charles at the time of his election, no subject of the Empire could be banned without a hearing. Charles ordered Luther to attend and issued him a safe-conduct. Fearing that Luther's eloquence might spread heresy among the great ones of the Empire, Aleander responded that Luther's crime was religious. He had already been found guilty by the Church, and secular authorities had no right to hear the case again. Charles withdrew the invitation. In the end Luther attended only because Charles and the papal envoy made a serious error. On 15 February they introduced a draft resolution declaring Luther an outlaw. The assembly erupted in violence, and to restore order, the estates were allowed to reply. It is a measure of Luther's popularity that within four days, the estates concluded that to deny him a hearing might provoke open revolt. They agreed, however, to support a ban if Luther refused to recant.

Luther appeared before the Diet on 17–18 April. After what appeared to be some initial hesitation, he issued his famous defiance: 'I cannot and will not recant, because it is neither safe nor wise to act against conscience. Here I stand, I can do no other. God help me! Amen.' Charles duly banned him on the following day, but the ban was never enforced. Frederick the Wise spirited his monk off to protective custody in the Wartburg, and after some months during which Luther translated the New Testament into German, he emerged to resume his duties at the University of Wittenburg. Frederick's motives in protecting Luther were complex and related more closely to his own Church and dynastic policies than to theology.[4] With his usual care, he did not state them openly, and seems never to have met the reformer in person. Charles, on the other hand, left no doubt about his views in the statement written in his own hand and read to the Diet on 19 April. After a brief discourse on the orthodoxy of his illustrious ancestors, he concluded:

> I am, therefore, resolved to maintain everything which these my forebearers have established to the present . . . It is certain that a single monk must err if his opinion his contrary to that of all Christendom. According to his opinion the whole of Christendom has been in error for a thousand years, and is continuing more so in that error in the present. To settle this matter I have resolved to stake upon this course my dominions and my possessions, my body and my soul. It would be a disgrace for me and for you, the noble and renowned German nation . . . as well as a perpetual stain upon ourselves and our posterity, if in this our day and generation, not only heresy but even the suspicion of heresy or the dimunition of our Christian religion were due to our negligence.
>
> After the impudent reply which Luther gave yesterday in the presence of us all, I now declare that I regret having delayed so long the proceedings against the aforementioned Luther and his false doctrine. I have now resolved never again, under any circumstances, to hear him. He is to be escorted home immediately . . . with due regard to the stipulations of his safe conduct. He is not to preach or seduce the people with his evil doctrine and not to incite them to rebellion.[5]

During the course of his long reign the Emperor would not waiver from this stance. He might compromise with Protestants on political matters, but he could not abandon his attachment to the Old Church without repudiating who and what he was. For Charles the outbreak of the Reformation was therefore a terrible misfortune. By dividing Germany, and in time the Netherlands, along religious lines, it made the already daunting goal of imperial unity even more difficult to achieve. The princes who accepted Luther's teachings gained from them an ideological basis for opposition to the Emperor and the opportunity to extract enormous wealth from confiscated Church properties. Within the Empire religious distrust made issues harder to resolve. In foreign policy Charles's rivals, notably the French and the Turks, gained from the Protestants a vital distraction and at times passive support for their struggles against him. There was far more to Charles's reign than religious struggle, but the problems bequeathed to him by Luther's revolt haunted it to the end.

For the moment, though, all was quiet. The condemnation of Luther had no immediate result, and Charles left Worms for the Netherlands. There he concluded an agreement whose impact on his realms would be second only to that of the Reformation. Charles's brother Ferdinand was born and raised in Spain. Charles had dispatched him to Brussels in 1517, probably because he feared his popularity with the Spanish, but it was now time to establish Ferdinand's position within the Empire. The catalyst was a marriage arranged years before by Maximilian. Ferdinand had been pledged to Anne, daughter of Vladislas, the Jagellonian King of Bohemia. A Habsburg–Jagellonian alliance was vital to Habsburg interests because it could ultimately bring them a rich kingdom whose ruler was also an imperial elector, but for five years the marriage had been delayed. Vladislas did not want to marry his daughter to someone with neither lands nor responsibilities. Charles and his counsellors had discussed the issue during the Diet of Worms, and concluded that Ferdinand should be given the ancestral Habsburg lands in Austria and southwest Germany. They may also have promised to have him named King of the Romans, or heir presumptive to the imperial title after Charles, but nothing was done about this for ten more years. Ferdinand married Anna in 1521 and the family agreement was announced publicly in the following year. Under its terms, Charles would remain the nominal ruler of the eastern lands, but Ferdinand would administer them on his behalf and be supported by their revenues. He would need them because the inexorable advance of the Ottoman Turks carried them further up the Danube valley with every passing year. In time they would be at the gates of Vienna.

Charles later regretted his generosity, but the terms of the compact were as momentous as they were irreversible. After Charles's death it would divide the Habsburg legacy and lay the foundations of not one, but two, great empires. The Spanish Habsburgs, descended from Charles, would rule Spain, the Netherlands, Italy, and the New World until 1700. The Austrian branch of the family, descended from Ferdinand, would long survive their Spanish cousins. They ruled Austria, Bohemia, and Hungary, and retained the imperial title until 1918.

In the midst of these negotiations Charles added to his future diplomatic capital by conceiving an illegitimate daughter, Margaret, who would become Duchess of Parma and then Regent of the Netherlands under Philip II. He returned to Spain in spring, 1522, after a brief stop in England to conclude the Treaty of Windsor with Henry VIII. Charles's presence in the Spanish kingdoms was long overdue. Adrian of Utrecht, as Regent in Charles's absence, had mishandled the early stages of the *comunero* revolt. By the end of August, 1520, 13 cities had joined the rebellion and proclaimed Queen Juana the legitimate ruler of Castile, a role that the Queen, with that strange passivity characteristic of her actions at this time, neither accepted nor rejected. Adrian remained a virtual prisoner at Valladolid. Far away in Germany, Charles knew that the survival of his throne depended upon the great nobles who until now had remained indifferent to the revolt. The *grandes* did not love Charles or his government, but as the *comunero* movement grew in strength, it became more radical and took on a populist tone that reflected the ancient antagonism between town and lordship. The lords became uneasy, and the risings known as the *germanías* of Valencia (1519–21), though unrelated to the revolt in Castile, may have increased their discomfort. A series of guild revolts fired in part by a desire for independence from Aragon and aggravated by Charles's failure to visit the kingdom, the *germanías* showed the Castilians how far social radicalism and millennial fantasies could go. When Charles appointed two of the *grandes*, Iñigo Velasco, Constable of Castile and the Admiral Fadrique Enríquez, Co-Regents in September, 1520, the nobles rallied to his cause. Adrian escaped from Valladolid, Tordesillas was retaken along with Queen Juana, and an army commanded by the Co-Regents shattered the main force of the *comuneros* at Villalar in April, 1521.

When Charles returned, then, the revolt was over, though Toledo continued to resist and the country as a whole seethed with resentment. It is a measure of how fast Charles had matured as a politician that he resolved to implement a program of reforms, some of which had been suggested by the rebels themselves. He would stay in Spain for the next seven years, learning the language and refining the instruments of government. In 1526 he married Isabella of Portugal, a choice as popular with his subjects as it was personally gratifying. Charles loved his wife deeply and did not remarry after her death in 1539. The royal couple spent much of their time at the Alhambra in Granada, while Charles enhanced his growing popularity by ruling as a true Spanish king. But if he avoided vindictive punishments and redressed many complaints, he did not consider reversing the verdict of Villalar. The towns, and by extension the Cortes, had lost. In all future dealings with the Crown, they would continue to supply money before their grievances would be heard, or as Charles put it to the first Cortes after his return, 'Yesterday

I asked you for funds; today I want your advice.'[6] Ironically, this principle became one of the foundation stones of Castile's dominant place within his Empire.

At the age of 22 Charles V had achieved control over a vast accumulation of territories including the Netherlands and Spain, with its dependencies in Italy and the Americas. In Germany his responsibilities as Emperor may have exceeded his resources, but he still possessed valuable assets in Austria and the German southwest. There had been nothing like it in Europe since the days of Charlemagne, but though Charles was Emperor, his patrimony was not an empire in the ordinary sense. It was a personal union of states that lacked either common institutions or territorial integrity. Defending it posed formidable problems. Distance alone imposed costs and difficulties. Moreover, his lands all but encircled France, a hostile kingdom with resources equal to his own. This meant that, strategically speaking, France occupied the geographic center of his territories, complicating logistics and ensuring that in the event of war he might be forced to fight on three fronts; four, if the Turks on his eastern borders became involved. Governance, too, posed obvious difficulties, but it is unwise to look at the Emperor's administrative problems from the standpoint of a modern territorial state. That concept was as yet in its infancy. Still less did he think in terms of the German nationalism that influenced so many nineteenth- and twentieth-century histories of his reign. But if Charles did not seek to mold his realms into a single state – or even to unify Germany – what was the basis of his policies?

Much has been written about Charles's theory of empire. In his early years he was guided by the Burgundian perspective of Chièvres, but it was obvious even before the Grand Chamberlain's death at the Diet of Worms that a pro-French policy oriented toward the interests of the Low Countries would not serve the needs of a larger empire. After 1521 Charles turned for advice to the Imperial Grand Chancellor, Mercurino de Gattinara. A Piedmontese lawyer, Gattinara had succeeded Jean de Sauvage after the latter's death in 1518. Gattinara's cosmopolitan perspective, no doubt influenced by his friendship with the humanist Erasmus, led him to embrace the concept of a universal empire. By this he meant a *universitas christiana* that would guarantee peace and tranquility in Europe while permitting concerted action against the Turks and Protestants. The term itself was coined by Gattinara's secretary, the Erasmian humanist Alonso de Valdés, and implied uniform policies toward those outside the Empire, but not a uniform system of government within it. Each component of the Empire would continue to be ruled according to its own laws and institutions.

Gattinara mentioned this concept to Charles in his communications and used it occasionally in imperial propaganda. It may have influenced the Chancellor's policies, which aimed at the isolation of France, the seizure of Milan, and territorial consolidation in the Netherlands, but it is not clear that the young Emperor took it seriously. Such a fantasy may have been attractive in the abstract and gratifying to the ego; as public relations, it was dangerous. It would be hard to imagine a theme that could provoke more fear among subjects and neighbors alike. French propaganda already invoked the imperial theme as a threat, and Charles's subjects, almost without exception, feared that being drawn into a worldwide empire would cost them their hard-won privileges and immunities. Moreover, in the absence of a financial system capable of allocating expenses and contributions among all of Charles's domains it is hard to imagine how such an empire might have worked.[7]

The Emperor's own understanding of his role was simpler and more traditional. Well aware of the sacral aspects of the imperial office and imbued with the principles of Burgundian chivalry, he believed that his primary duties as Emperor were to foster peace among Christians and to advance the faith. His concept of the latter drew heavily upon the medieval crusading tradition. When he became King of Spain in 1516, he adopted his famous personal device: the motto *Plus Oultre* ('Yet Further') above a representation of the Pillars of Hercules. It referred, not to conquests as yet unmade in the New World, but to the task of carrying Christianity into Africa as a logical extension of the Spanish *reconquista*. As Emperor, he added to this the responsibilty for protecting central Europe against the Turk. The two tasks were compatible, though they pertained to different offices. After 1521, the idea of peace among Christians included healing the religious schism begun by Luther.

Throughout his reign, Charles tried in this sense to act as the champion of Christendom. When circumstances permitted, he confronted *al-Islam*. He sometimes justified his policies in Italy and Germany as peace-making among Christians, and dreamed at times of uniting the ruling dynasties of Europe through intermarriage. He did not, however, elevate these thoughts into a general theory of empire. At Worms Charles invoked the idea of 'one lord alone, as is the custom of the Holy Roman Empire,' and referred to imperial ideals in his call for a general council of the Church (Madrid, 16 September 1529).[8] By this he was clearly referring to the Holy Roman Empire of the German Nation, as it was called in Germany, and not to the realms that lay outside the provisions of its constitution. Otherwise, he remained silent on this and all other theoretical matters.

Pragmatic and suspicious of high-sounding theories, Charles understood his responsibilities but never forgot that his primary obligation was always to the dynastic interests of his family. The need to preserve every square yard of the Habsburg patrimony regardless of the cost in blood or money is a constant theme in his letters to his son. Marital diplomacy as a means of retaining or expanding that patrimony remained a central feature of his policies, and he always claimed the right to dispose of his inheritance as he wished. This was because, like other princes of the age, Charles tended to think of his hereditary lands and titles as personal property. If he sometimes used Spanish resources to support his goals as Emperor of Germany, it was not because Spain was part of the Holy Roman Empire but because its wealth was his to use. The Emperor understood national feeling and occasionally referred to the national characteristics of his subjects. He was also aware that they would defend their customs, rights, and privileges to the bitter end whenever they were challenged. From his perspective it was therefore both unnecessary and undesirable to weld his realms into a single state. He attempted to improve administration in each of the states he ruled, but forged no common institutions that might form the basis of a government that would embrace them all.

When Gattinara died in 1530, Charles allowed the office of Grand Chancellor to lapse. Never again would his councils be dominated by one great servant whose office derived not only from the Emperor's favor but from imperial precedent. He would have other diplomatic advisors, notably Nicholas Perrenot de Granvelle, an able lawyer from the Franche-Comté who inherited some of Gattinara's responsibilities as Keeper of the Seals and became the Emperor's secretary for northern European affairs, and Perrenot's son, Anton, who would become Bishop of Arras and Cardinal Granvelle before continuing his career under Philip II. For the most part, however, Charles would make policy himself. He was not averse to consultation. He regularly sought the opinion of his secretaries, his military commanders, his family, and his confessor. He heard the complaints and suggestions of officials at every level and sometimes acted on them, but he never acquired a 'prime minister' or favorite, nor did he seek to develop an Empire-wide administration. After 1530, the only unity among his far-flung possessions was provided by the Emperor himself.

After 1530 the Emperor's policies, too, would be largely reactive and uninformed by principles that did not relate to dynastic survival or religious orthodoxy. In this he had little choice. His realms would be under almost constant attack from France, the Turks, and their North African allies, and he believed firmly that to sacrifice any one of them would endanger the whole. Meanwhile, Germany would be convulsed by the Reformation, a movement that he could neither accept nor defeat. Though Charles and his administrators collected and spent vast sums, they could never meet all of the obligations incurred in these struggles, nor could they bring them to an acceptable conclusion. From their perspective the reign became largely a holding action, a defense of inherited property and the ancestral faith. Its failures and achievements should be understood in that context.

2

THE EMPIRE DEFENDED

Charles V spent much of his reign at war. Contemporaries said that when in the field lethargy and reticence deserted him, his spirits lifted, and he became involved in every detail of military life. Most of them thought him a capable general, but if Charles was a warrior by temperament, he was no warmonger. From his perspective, war was forced upon him by others. The ongoing conflicts of his reign were three: the wars with France, the confrontation with Islam, and the complex struggle against Protestantism and the princes of the Empire. Each involved different enemies with different goals. Sometimes they found ways to combine against him, but cultural differences and other problems of communication ensured that their periods of collaboration would be sporadic and often ineffective. Nevertheless, the simultaneous existence of such varied threats dissipated the Emperor's resources and prevented him from acting in one area without considering the effect of his policies on the other two. He could rarely afford to think of these problems in isolation, but narrative clarity and the enormous differences among his enemies encourage us to examine each threat independently.

THE STRUGGLE AGAINST FRANCE

In terms of blood and money the most costly of these conflicts was the protracted quarrel with France, sometimes known as the Habsburg–Valois rivalry. Campaigns against Francis I and his son, Henry II, consumed 16 years of the reign and continued until the year after Charles's death. After that, civil war within France prevented the resumption of hostilities until the Spanish invasion of 1592, but while the Emperor lived, France remained his greatest rival and the chief obstacle to his ambitions.

The wars between Charles V and Francis I continued a struggle that had begun in 1494 with the invasion of Italy by Charles VIII of France. The French King claimed Naples on the basis of his descent from René of Anjou. René had been deposed as King of Naples by Alfonso V of Aragon, who became Alfonso I of Naples in 1443. Alfonso's heirs, the descendants of his illegitimate son and cousins of Ferdinand of Aragon, had now ruled Naples for more than 50 years, but the long-dormant French claim was encouraged by a faction of Neapolitan nobles and by the Duke of Milan who was then engaged in a dispute with Alfonso II. Realizing that Italy, with its dozens of weak and contentious states was a power vacuum waiting to be filled, Charles VIII entered the peninsula at the head of a great army. He managed to take Naples, but the Italian states formed the League of Venice and drove him out of the country in 1495. After his death in 1498 his successor, Louis XII, continued the struggle in the face of determined opposition from Ferdinand of Aragon. Posing as his family's champion, Ferdinand restored them to the throne in 1495. Then, in 1500 he agreed to divide the kingdom with Louis XII. Federico, the last survivor of the cadet branch of the Aragonese royal house, went into comfortable exile in France. The final act of this convoluted drama took place in 1504 when the Spanish army drove the French out of Naples and Ferdinand had himself proclaimed King in his own right.

The central issue in Italian politics now became control of Milan. Citing hereditary claims based on his descent from Valentina Viscontini (d. 1408) and Louis of Orléans, Louis XII had seized Milan from the incumbent Sforzas in 1499. He lost it again in 1512 when a coalition of powers organized by Pope Julius II and reinforced by the Spanish army drove the French from Italy. When Francis I came to the throne in 1515 he inaugurated his reign by retaking Milan and personally defending it at the battle of Marignano. At the same time he brought Genoa into the French orbit and expelled its doge, primarily to secure the approaches to Milan.

French policy does not at this time appear to have been inspired by broad geopolitical concerns. If Francis I and his advisers, like French statesmen of a later age, feared encirclement by the Habsburgs, they never mentioned it. Their specific actions were based on the King's understanding of his hereditary rights, his desire to please the nobility of the realm by enriching them through war, and a growing sense of personal rivalry with Charles that had begun with the imperial election.[1] If anything, it was Charles, under the influence of Gattinara's imperial ideals, who had begun to think in broader, more 'modern' terms. Because the two halves of Charles's territories were divided by France, Gattinara believed that Milan would have to serve as the strategic center of his Empire, linking Spain and southern Italy with the north. Only then could troop movements and communications be secured. The alternative involved a long journey by sea through the hazarous waters of the Bay of Biscay and the English Channel where imperial ships could easily be intercepted by the French. If a justification for the recovery of Milan were needed, Charles could claim that the city had always been part of the Empire and that its Duke, Francesco Maria Sforza, was his vassal who had been wrongfully dispossessed by the French. Gattinara's thinking on this point presages that of Philip II and marks the origin of what would become the 'Spanish Road,' the always threatened but vital lifeline connecting Spain to the Netherlands.

France, however, began the war of 1521–22. The months after the imperial election had been filled with diplomatic maneuvering. Francis knew that Charles had met with Henry VIII of England a month before the inconclusive Anglo-French conference at the Field of Cloth of Gold (June–July, 1520), and feared that England might be thrown into the balance against him. He also knew that Charles's agents were negotiating a treaty with Pope Leo X by which an Italian league would help Charles gain Milan while the Pope took Parma, Piacenza, and Ferrara. Fearing the worst, Francis embarked on a series of pre-emptive strikes. To distract Charles from Italy, a French army invaded Navarre, hoping that the *comunero* revolt then raging in Castile would inhibit the Spanish defense. On the borders of the Netherlands, the Duke of Gelre, acting with French support and taking advantage of local discontent, seized Friesland, Groningen, and Overijssel. Another French surrogate, Robert de la Marck, Lord of Sedan, invaded Luxemburg.

Charles was now faced with war on three fronts, but things went well for him from the first. In Spain, the Battle of Villalar ended the *comunero* revolt in April, 1521, before the French could enter Pamplona on 19 May. The Spanish army, undistracted by rebellion, required little more than a month to drive them from Navarre. In the Netherlands, Charles's troops seized Tournai and incorporated it, together with its bishopric, into his empire. They then drove the Duke of Gelre from the northeast, paving the way for Charles to annex Friesland in 1523–24. Meanwhile, the schemes of Robert de la Marck in Luxemburg came to nothing. This series of French failures enabled Charles to begin a process of territorial consolidation in the Netherlands that would continue throughout his reign. After taking Friesland and Tournai he used French aggression as an excuse to detach Flanders and Artois from the jurisdiction of the Parlement of Paris, placing them under the Great Council of Mechelen. On the Italian front a papal–imperial army, heavily reinforced by troops from the kingdom of Naples, seized Milan and restored Doge Antonio Adorno to his post at Genoa. A French attempt to relieve Milan met with bloody defeat at the Battle of La Bicocca in April, 1522.

Francis did not respond to these losses until late in 1524, in part because he was distracted by the rebellion of Charles de Bourbon, Constable of France. Angered by the escheat of his late wife's estate to the Crown, Bourbon eventually deserted to the imperial side and became one of Charles's commanders in Italy. When the invasion came, Francis led it himself. He managed to retake Milan in October, 1524, but on Charles's birthday, 24 February, 1525, imperial forces commanded by Bourbon and Lannoy, a Burgundian noble close to Charles, destroyed the French army in a hunting park outside Pavia and captured the King. The Emperor, who had returned to Spain in 1522 and would remain there until 1529, was not present.

The imperial victory stunned Europe, but Charles in the end gained little from it. He brought Francis to Spain as a prisoner and persuaded him to sign the Treaty of Madrid (January, 1526) by which the King agreed to abandon all claims in Italy and the Netherlands and to surrender Burgundy in return for his freedom. His two sons would be held hostage in Spain, but there was no other guarantee of performance beyond the King's word. Chancellor Gattinara was outraged at this apparent naiveté. In an act of extraordinary disobedience he refused to fix the imperial seal to the document because it was in his view unenforceable. This action did not invalidate the treaty, but Francis, claiming duress, repudiated the agreement as soon as he returned to France. Gattinara no doubt thought himself vindicated, but though Charles seems to have accepted the lack of guarantees out of chivalric regard for a gentleman's word and because his confessor advised it, in practical terms he had few alternatives. The hostage provision, of course, was meaningless. Charles would have no use for the boys if Francis defaulted, and the King assumed correctly that he could ransom them at a later date. At the same time, Charles could not hold the King in Madrid forever. Whatever Gattinara might have thought, it is hard to imagine enforcing such a treaty under any circumstances as long as the Kingdom of France retained the capacity to make war.

Within weeks it became obvious that the chief result of Pavia had been to frighten the states of northern Italy, who now feared that the Emperor would end by controlling the entire peninsula. Charles's former tutor Adrian of Utrecht had been elected Pope in January, 1522, but died after a pontificate of little more than a year. Though less malleable than Charles had hoped, he had at least refused to ally with the French. His successor, the Medici Pope Clement VII (1523–34) held different views. Clement, together with Venice, Florence, and even Francesco Maria Sforza, who had been restored at Milan by Charles after the Battle of Bicocca, joined France in the League of Cognac (May, 1526) to preserve 'the liberty of Milan and Italy.' There was no immediate French invasion of Italy because Francis needed time to muster his resources. Taking advantage of the delay, Charles tried to put pressure on the Pope by stirring up a revolt in the Roman Campagna. The tactic backfired. A papal army defeated the rebels who, in desperation, called upon Bourbon, the imperial commander at Milan, for help. The Constable descended upon Rome, but died in the assault. His troops, unpaid, starving, and freed of the restraints of command, sacked the Holy City in May, 1527, committing innumerable atrocities and forcing the Pope to take refuge in the Castel de Sant' Angelo where he remained a virtual prisoner for nine months. The Sack of Rome by an imperial army was as great a sensation as the victory at Pavia and a scandal of historic proportions, but like Pavia it changed little. The Pope's misfortunes did not deter the League of Cognac, while a skillful propaganda campaign allowed Charles, who had not authorized the attack and apologized profusely, to avert much of the blame for the atrocities at Rome.

The Sack of Rome may have influenced Clement's decision to equivocate on another great issue of the day, but even that is questionable. Henry VIII of England, unaware that German and Spanish soldiers were at that moment rampaging through the streets of Rome, chose May of 1527 to petition Clement for a divorce from Catherine of Aragon, his wife of 18 years and the aunt of Charles V. Charles, of course, bitterly opposed what he saw as an insult to his family. Clement could not have granted Henry's request while a virtual prisoner of the Emperor, but the King's Great Matter was problematic on other grounds. The petitions themselves were ineptly drawn and based on contradictory arguments. Experts on canon law could not accept them as written, and Clement could not understand why Henry was bothering him with such a question in the first place. He believed, perhaps rightly, that Henry's chief minister, Cardinal Wolsey, had the right to grant the needed dispensations in his capacity as Archbishop of York.[2] To make matters worse, news of the Sack reached England before Wolsey could leave for Rome. The Cardinal, whose ambitions were limitless, hatched a scheme by which Clement would, in addition to approving the divorce, allow Wolsey to exercise papal powers from Avignon during the Pope's captivity. Clement's reaction to this may be imagined. Even after his release in December, 1527, he refused to cooperate. When Clement allied himself with the Emperor in 1530, the case became hopeless. Thwarted in his desires both political and personal, Henry began the long process of separating England from the Catholic Church.

Meanwhile, the war in Italy continued. In August, 1527, a French army invaded Lombardy, isolating Milan and forcing Genoa once again to abandon the imperial cause. In the next year, Charles denounced Francis for breaking the Treaty of Madrid and issued a formal challenge to Francis to settle their differences in single combat. He was apparently sincere in this as his family was very much alarmed,[3] but Francis, though at least equal to Charles as an athlete, refused to participate. From the Papal States the French then entered the kingdom of Naples in February, 1528. Their new ally, the Genoese Admiral Andrea Doria, blockaded the city's port after defeating an imperial fleet commanded by Philibert of Orange, a childhood companion of Charles who was now Viceroy of Naples. It appeared certain that Naples would fall, but French resources were by this time stretched to the limit. In August, 1528, Doria abandoned his blockade, having been won over again to the imperial side by what amounted to bribes. The French, short of supplies and suffering from an epidemic of cholera, retreated. In the following year another French attack on Milan was crushed by the Spanish General Antonio de Leyva at the Battle of Landriano. Francis was now left without a credible army in Italy.

The Peace of Cambrai, which ended the war of 1527–29, lasted seven years. Called the Ladies' Peace, it was negotiated in private by the Regent of the Netherlands, Margaret of Austria, and the French Queen-Mother, Louise of Savoy. Francis agreed to abandon his claims to Milan, Naples, Flanders, and Artois and to cede Tournai to the Emperor. Charles gave up his cherished, if unenforceable, claim to Burgundy. Painful as this may have been for Charles, he clearly gained more than he lost. Moreover, he, too, needed peace. His resources, like those of

Francis I, were depleted, and he feared correctly that the Ottoman Turks were preparing an assault on the Habsburg lands in Austria. He also needed time to consolidate his gains in the Low Countries and Italy. Taking advantage of the French collapse after Landriano, Charles restored the Medici to Florence, earning the gratitude of the Medici Pope, Clement VII, and ensuring that for the rest of the century and beyond Florence would remain a protectorate of the Empire and later of Spain. Clement, in turn, Crowned Charles Holy Roman Emperor and King of Italy at Bologna on 24 February, 1530, his thirtieth birthday and the fifth anniversary of the Battle of Pavia. At the same time Charles restored Francesco Sforza at Milan. When Sforza died without heirs in 1535, the Emperor asserted what he believed to be his historic rights and assumed direct rule over the city, governing it thereafter through a lieutenant general while preserving the city's parliament and other local institutions.

The spectacle of Charles strengthening his position in Italy over seven long years was more than the King of France could bear. With Sforza dead, he revived his claim to Milan. In 1536 Francis attacked Piedmont and Savoy in violation of the Peace of Cambrai. He hoped to advance on Milan, but his forces became bogged down in a struggle for Turin and failed to penetrate Lombardy. Once again, Charles challenged his enemy to single combat. The Emperor's persistence in issuing these challenges indicates the degree to which he, and perhaps some of his contemporaries, were still captivated by chivalric ideals, but if so, their attachments were no longer universally shared. To everyone's relief the new Pope, Paul III (1534–49), forbade all discussion of a duel. Instead, the Emperor, commanding in person, devastated Provence without achieving his objective, the seizure of Marseilles.

He then returned to Spain, but the French renewed their attacks on the southern borders of the Netherlands in the spring of 1537. Margaret of Austria had died in 1531. Her successor as Regent, Charles's sister Mary of Hungary, lacked Margaret's tact and diplomatic touch but proved to be a formidable organizer of war. The French campaign caused widespread devastation while stretching the resources of both governments to their limits. Otherwise, it accomplished little. A temporary truce arranged at Bomy in June, 1537, broadened into a general peace brokered by Charles's oldest sister, Queen Eleanor of France, and the Pope. After much preliminary negotiation, Charles and Francis personally ratified the agreement at Aigues Mortes, a small village amid the lagoons at the mouth of the Rhone. Setting aside the fears of his counsellors, Charles accepted the King's invitation to return to the Netherlands by way of France and travelled the length of the country as an honored guest in 1539. For Charles, the joy of the occasion was marred by the death of the Empress Isabella on 1 May, 1539, from the complications of childbirth. She had given him three children, Mary, Philip, and Juana. Four others, including the last, did not survive. Though deeply affected by his loss, Charles knew that he could not reject French hospitality. The visit, enlivened by chivalric spectacle on the grandest scale, proceeded as planned.

The cordiality evident in the Emperor's grand tour lasted less than three years. In 1541 Charles used his respite from the French to launch an attack on Muslim Algiers with disastrous results. In 1542 France launched a three-pronged offensive against his lands. The Duke of Guise besieged Perpignan as a preliminary to invading Catalonia, but was driven off by the Duke of Alba, a young commander who would play a growing role in the military affairs of the reign and beyond. A more senior Spanish commander, the Marquis del Vasto, thwarted the last French attempt on Milan, but in the Netherlands a force raised by Duke William of Cleves and supported by the French penetrated to the walls of Antwerp and Louvain. Cleves had become Duke of Gelre after Charles of Egmond's death in 1538, and had inherited both his grievances against the Emperor and the services of Gelre's fierce and capable Marshal, Martin van Rossem. Only a spirited defense by townspeople, and in the case of Louvain, by university students, prevented disaster.

The year ended with the astonishing spectacle of the Turkish fleet wintering at Toulon. French diplomats had long been active at Constantinople, for the French and the Ottomans had in Charles V a common enemy. Until the Emperor's attack on Algiers, they had failed to coordinate their efforts. Fortunately for Charles and his subjects, the Turkish fleet accomplished little in 1542–43, and the chief effect of this scandalous alliance between the Muslim infidel and the most Christian King of France was to galvanize opinion in the Holy Roman Empire. In a burst of unaccustomed generosity, the Imperial Diet granted Charles 24 000 infantry and 6000 cavalry for the campaign of 1543. Once again assuming personal command of his army, the Emperor attacked Cleves and captured its Duke, who was happy to cede Gelre and Zutphen to Charles while retaining his other possessions. Charles then invaded France while Henry VIII of England, with whom he had been conniving since 1541, attacked Boulogne. Charles marched as far as Meaux.

There he learned that the Parisians had begun to evacuate their city, but the campaign foundered when Henry refused to join him in assaulting Paris. Francis regrouped and it was not until 1544 that the two sides agreed to negotiate after the last French attempt on Naples ended in a pyrrhic victory at Ceresole. The French were left in possession of the field, but had experienced such heavy casualties that they could not continue the campaign. For all practical purposes, the Italian phase of the wars was over.

The failure of Francis I to make good his claims in Italy left Charles the dominant force in the peninsula. At the beginning of the wars, Charles ruled Naples, Sicily, and Sardinia. By 1535 he had secured Milan and brought Florence and Genoa securely into his orbit. The papacy was for a time, at least, neutralized and Venice, long suspicious of imperial power, had accepted the inevitable. The reasons for the Emperor's success were chiefly military. The French army was superior in heavy cavalry and at least equal to the imperial forces in artillery. Its infantry, on the other hand, suffered from critical deficiencies. France had no adequately trained native foot soldiers and relied upon Swiss mercenaries, who, though formidable when paid, remained wedded to the pike tactics that had served them so well in the preceding century. They therefore lacked the tactical flexibility of the Spanish units or even of the German *Landsknechte* who normally served the Emperor as mercenaries. The Spanish, though they rarely numbered more than a fifth of the imperial combatants, had long since mastered the coordination of pikes with shot. In 1536 Charles formed them into the *tercios* that would dominate European battlefields until the Thirty Years' War (1618–48). These units, nominally of 3000 men, combined pikes and arquebuses in varying proportions according to need. By the 1520s *Landsknecht* units supplied by military contracters were normally supported by arquebusiers as well. From Bicocca on, the superiority of imperial infantry prevailed, the Swiss lost much of their effectiveness, and Charles's men won most of the battles.

Equally important was the fact that since the beginning of the wars, an increasing number of cities and strong points in northern Italy were refortified using the recently developed bastion trace. This new system, based upon low but massive walls whose every surface could be covered by flanking fire from angled bastions, provided an effective defense against the French artillery whose successes in the early phase of the Italian wars had inspired it. Cities like Milan became invulnerable to short sieges, while the sheer density of fortification in the north Italian plain slowed campaigns to a crawl. The proliferation of citadels may also have served as a check on local populations whose passions might lead them to welcome an invader.[4]

With France exhausted and Charles firmly in control of the Italian peninsula, negotiations resumed. The Peace of Crépy (19 September, 1544) was a serious attempt to end the Habsburg–Valois struggles, but Charles's motive in signing it remains something of a mystery. It is generally thought that he wanted the freedom to act against the Lutherans in Germany at almost any price. If this is true, he may have gone too far. Had they been implemented, the terms he accepted at Crépy would have squandered the fruits of 20 years of warfare at a time when, in hindsight at least, victory was assured.

The Emperor agreed to a matrimonial alliance by which Francis's youngest son, the Duke of Orleáns, was given a choice of brides. If he married Charles's daughter, Mary, he would receive the Netherlands when Charles died. If he chose the Emperor's niece, Anne of Hungary, he could have Milan within a year. Francis, in turn, would give up his personal claims to the Netherlands and Naples. These alternatives provoked furious debate among the Emperor's counsellors. Ironically, Alba, who would one day be charged with putting down the Netherlands revolt, wanted to keep Milan as the cornerstone of a Mediterranean empire and let the Low Countries go. Most of the Spanish agreed. The Germans and the Netherlanders wanted to abandon Milan, but in the end the Peace of Crépy, like its predecessors, accomplished little.[5] Orleáns died in 1545, and a grateful Charles wrote in his *Memorias*: 'This death came just in time, and, being a natural one, it could be said that God had sent it to accomplish his secret designs.'[6] Francis followed his youngest son to the grave in 1547. The final conflicts between Charles and Francis's successor, Henry II, began five years later and ended only after the Emperor's death. They were closely related, however, to the developing struggle within the Empire and are best understood as part of Charles's conflict with the German Protestants.

The wars with France consumed Charles's best energies and a disproportionate share of his treasure. From his perspective, they were defensive in character and a distraction that prevented him from dealing effectively with the two problems closest to his heart: the Turks and Protestants. He even failed to regain Burgundy. Yet if the French wars mired him in disputes that he would have preferred to avoid and contributed greatly to the financial debacle at the end of his reign, they also brought him great benefits. His victories over Francis and his surrogates in the Netherlands enabled Charles to consolidate his territories there and strengthen their institutions in ways that would otherwise have been impossible. More dramatically, it brought him effective control over the Italian peninsula. After the Emperor's death, Milan passed to his Spanish heirs, who also retained his special relationships with Genoa and Florence. Italy from the reign of Charles V to the end of the seventeenth century would remain for all practical purposes a Spanish dependency.

The impact of the wars on France is harder to assess. Their enormous cost placed great demands on the French taxpayer, encouraged inflation, and led Francis I to adopt the sale of offices on an unprecedented scale. Fiscal and administrative reforms designed primarily to help pay for the wars bred discontent by threatening long-established local privileges. At the same time, the government could do little to ease the reintegration of French soldiers into civilian life after each war. The social dislocation that resulted from these changes may not have caused the civil wars that convulsed France from 1561 to 1594, but it certainly contributed to them. From the Habsburg point of view the French civil wars were, of course, good because they neutralized what had become the dynasty's greatest enemy for more than 30 years. But France was large and rich and would eventually recover. When it did so with a vengeance in the seventeenth century, the old rivalries began anew. Francis I may not have thought in terms of encirclement; Richelieu, a careful student of history, did. By this time the Austrian and Spanish descendants of Charles V had long been separated, but Richelieu could not ignore the possibility of Habsburg collusion. His fears became manifest in 1618 when an Austrian attack on Bohemia coincided with the Spanish invasion of the Palatinate. It was the beginning of the Thirty Years' War and raised the spectre of Habsburg hegemony in Europe. For the remainder of his life, the great minister of Louis XIII pursued an anti-Habsburg policy with remarkable success. The threat, however, was less dire than he imagined. Cooperation between the Spanish and Austrian Habsburgs was never perfect and rarely directed primarily against France. Still, the legacy of Charles V had created the *appearance* of a mortal threat by encirclement and neither the Cardinal nor his successors could ignore it. Years later, Louis XIV based his policies on similar assumptions and plunged Europe into a series of wars aimed at protecting his frontiers against Habsburg encroachment. The historic rivalry between France and Germany may therefore be seen, at least in part, as a consequence of Charles's reign.

THE TURKISH THREAT

Vast, exotic, and above all non-Christian, the Ottoman Empire haunted the imaginations of sixteenth-century Europeans. Their misconceptions about it were legion, but the threat it posed to Europe's eastern and southern frontiers was real. Beginning in the thirteenth century as one of several *ghazi* principalities which supported themselves and advanced the cause of Islam by raiding their Christian neighbors, the Ottomans had expanded relentlessly in Anatolia and the Balkans until, in 1453, they captured the great city of Constantinople and put an end to a thousand years of Byzantine history. After a half-century of consolidation, a new offensive under Sultan Selim I 'the Grim' defeated the Mamluks and doubled the Empire by adding Egypt, Syria, and southwestern Anatolia in 1516–17. After Selim's death in 1520 his son Suleyman, known in the west as 'the Magnificent,' began a long advance up the Danube valley. At the Battle of Mohács in 1526 his forces destroyed the Hungarian army and killed Louis, King of Bohemia and Hungary, and husband of the Emperor's sister Mary. The Turks then occupied central Hungary, which placed them within striking distance of Vienna, capital of the Habsburg ancestral lands.

The invasion of Hungary affronted Christendom and created a potential threat to the Empire. By trying to reap personal advantage from the loss, Charles's brother, the Archduke Ferdinand, made that threat immediate. Ferdinand was married to Anne, sister of the late King Louis. He immediately claimed that this marriage gave him the hereditary right to rule both Hungary and Bohemia, though as he well knew the two monarchies had long been elective. Predictably, the Bohemian and Hungarian Diets rejected Ferdinand's claims on constitutional grounds, but the Bohemians nevertheless elected him King in October, 1526. The Hungarian situation was more complicated. John Zápolya, Voivod of Transylvania and an ally of the Turks, contested Ferdinand's election. When bribery and intrigue failed to secure the throne for Ferdinand, he declared Zápolya a rebel and in 1527 occupied Croatia, Slovenia, and western Hungary. Suleyman responded by placing Transylvania under his protection.

Ferdinand was now the elected King of Bohemia and in possession of the western third of Hungary, but he had stirred up a hornet's nest in eastern Europe. King Sigismund of Poland supported his son-in-law Zápolya, a Turkish client, and Turks, Poles, and Transylvanians became the *de facto* allies of Francis I. Ferdinand, now virtually isolated, hoped for assistance from the princes of the Empire, but the religious issue intervened. Several of the German princes had by this time declared their support for the Reformation, and the devout Ferdinand demanded a strong pro-Catholic resolution from the Diet of Speyer. His intransigeance used up what political capital he possessed. The Catholic majority passed his edict but, having offended their reformed colleagues at Ferdinand's insistence, would send him no money. The offended minority rejected his pleas as well. Charles was not amused. At his urging Ferdinand sent a peace mission to Suleyman, but then overplayed his hand by demanding the return of those parts of Hungary that had been seized by the Turks.

On 27 September, 1529 Suleyman besieged Vienna with perhaps 100 000 troops. The Emperor, entangled in the last phases of the Italian war of 1527–29, could not come in person, nor could he send men or money. His one contribution was to extort a monetary contribution from those German princes who were now called Protestants after their formal objection or protest against the edict of Speyer. Charles told them that if they did not pay, he would return to Germany and deal with the religious question himself as soon as he settled with France. They paid to avoid a confrontation, but did not send troops. Ferdinand and his unimpressive force of about 20 000 men were on their own. Fortunately, Suleyman's horses lacked adequate fodder and the autumn weather had turned difficult. He withdrew on 14 October.

Vienna withstood a second Turkish advance in 1532. This time the Emperor, unencumbered by a war with France, commanded in person, but there was no battle before the walls of Vienna. Heroic resistance by the tiny fortress of Güns near the border of Hungary and Styria delayed the Turkish advance for much of August. Once again short of supplies and facing the prospect of a central European winter, Suleyman decided to withdraw. A German force engaged his rearguard successfully on 13 September, but aside from the usual skirmishing there were no further actions. The Turks would not return to Vienna for more than a century and a half.

In the end Vienna remained safe because it was just beyond the reach of Ottoman logistics. Turkish armies were large, typically numbering three times as many combatants as their Christian counterparts. Even with the development of a permanent base on the lower Danube, it proved impossible to bring such a force into position before the last days of the campaigning season. At the same time, Ferdinand could make little progress of his own against the Ottomans in central Hungary. His revenues were inadequate to the task, and anti-Habsburg feeling within the Imperial Diet, to say nothing of the tensions created by the Reformation, made raising money from that source extremely difficult. Charles could provide little more than moral support. Though personally committed to the crusade against the Turk, he had mortgaged his own resources for the wars with France. To Ferdinand, Charles sometimes appeared indifferent to happenings on the Empire's eastern front, but the Emperor understood the strategic implications of Suleyman's retreats as well as the propaganda value of the Turkish menace in dealing with the Protestants of the Empire. His caution, if unworthy of the crusading spirit, was based on an accurate appraisal of the Ottoman threat to central Europe.

Ferdinand accepted the limitations of his circumstances as he was so often forced to do. In 1533 he abandoned his claims to Turkish Hungary and recognized Zápolya as an Ottoman vassal. Ironically, when Zápolya died in 1540 he unexpectedly left Transylvania to Ferdinand in violation of his agreement with the Turks. Ferdinand, however, failed to occupy his new possession, and Suleyman assumed direct Ottoman control of Transylvania as Regent for the Voivod's infant son, John Sigismund. During the next six years, Suleyman extended his personal control over Buda and those parts of central Hungary that he had conquered in 1526. The truce of 1547 secured this region for the Turks, granted western Hungary to Ferdinand in return for an annual tribute, and established Transylvania as an autonomous state under Turkish rule. The tripartite division of Hungary, like Vienna's immunity from Turkish attack, would last until 1683.

The second and, from the perspective of Charles's own subjects, more serious Turkish threat came in the Mediterranean. In 1522 an Ottoman fleet took Rhodes and evicted its garrison of Knights Hospitalers. Charles eventually resettled the Knights at Malta from which they conducted piratical raids against Muslim interests, but the greatest problem facing the Emperor involved not the Turkish fleet itself but its allies, the Barbary pirates. Muslim pirates from the towns of the North African coast, reinforced by Morisco refugees from the religious policies of Ferdinand and Isabella, had raided the coasts of Spain and Italy for years seeking booty and slaves, who could be ransomed for cash or put to work in the North African economy if no ransom were forthcoming. Ferdinand of Aragon had pursued an aggressive policy against them by establishing garrisons in the coastal towns of the Maghrib. He took Melilla in 1497 and Peñón de la Gómera, Oran, Bugia, and Tripoli between 1508 and 1511, but could do nothing to develop a Spanish presence in the surrounding countryside. The Aragonese *presidios* remained fragile enclaves on the edges of a hostile Muslim world.

At about the same time a group of Levantine corsairs led by Aroudj Re'is and his brothers, Isaac and Kheir-ed-din, began to establish a formidable reputation in the western Mediterranean. The hard-pressed townsmen of the Maghrib welcomed them as allies, and in 1516, the year of Ferdinand's death, the pirates established themselves in force at Algiers. Charles's new government moved swiftly against them and mounted an expeditionary force that managed to kill both Aroudj and Isaac. Kheir-ed-din, realizing that he was as yet no match for the Spanish, placed Algiers and himself under the Sultan's protection in return for military assistance. Algiers became an autonomous western *sanjac* or province of the Ottoman Empire, reinforced by 2000 janissaries, 4000 other Turkish troops, and their artillery. A second Christian expedition under the Viceroy of Naples failed to dislodge them, and for the next decade Kheir-ed-din, known to the west as Barbarossa for his flaming red beard, ravaged the coasts of Spain and Italy with near impunity. From the beginning of his reign, Charles's subjects pressed him to do something about it.

The Ladies' Peace of 1529 and the retreat of the Turks before Vienna in 1532 seemed to offer him an opportunity for action. The Emperor's Genoese allies seized Patras as a diversion in 1532, and in 1533 took Coron in the Peloponnesos as well. The Sultan responded by enlisting the Algerian pirate fleet. In 1534 Barbarossa launched a raid on Italy that brought him close to Rome itself and captured Tunis from its Bey, Muley Hassan, a Spanish ally. The imperialists prudently withdrew from Coron, but the seizure of Tunis could not be ignored. The city, with its vast harbor that had once supported the fleets of Carthage, lies only 24 hours by galley from the Sicilian coast. To Charles the moment seemed propitious. For once he was undistracted by other military obligations and his war chest was swollen by the first windfall from Pizarro's conquest of Peru, 800 000 ducats of which were confiscated by royal *cédula* in return for bonds or *juros* of 3 percent. In 1535 Charles, commanding in person, launched a massive amphibious assault that restored Muley Hassan and forced Barbarossa back to his lair at Algiers.

The Tunis campaign was an enormous success, but it did not end the North African threat. Charles lacked the resources to move against Algiers, and Barbarossa spent the next two years savaging the Balearic Islands, the Valencian coast, and southern Italy. In the meantime,

France concluded its first formal alliance with the Ottoman Empire in 1536 and started the war that ended with Charles's unsuccessful campaign in Provence. Nothing could be done about Barbarossa until the truce of 1538 ended the French conflict and left Charles free to conclude a naval alliance with Venice and the Papacy. Then, in September of that year, Barbarossa defeated the combined forces of this league at Prevesa, one of the greatest naval battles of the sixteenth century. The alliance dissolved, but financial exhaustion would have prevented further action in any case. Years of warfare had strained the Emperor's finances – and the patience of his subjects – to breaking point. From 1538 to 1540 protests against the heavy taxation needed to pay for the wars with France led to plots and disorders in the Netherlands that culminated in open revolt at Ghent. In 1540 the Viceroy of Naples, Pedro de Toledo, declared that taxation had reduced his subjects to the level of 'brute animals' and refused to honor imperial bills of exchange drawn on Neapolitan revenues. Even the Cortes of Castile rejected the Emperor's request for a *sisa*, or tax on foodstuffs. There were no more windfalls from Peru. The last sequestration of the Inca's treasure had been used against France in 1538 and the *hacienda* of Castile had to float a giro of 150 000 ducats just to pay the garrison of La Goletta, the fortress that controlled the harbor of Tunis.

Charles spent the winter of 1540–41 at Regensburg, trying to reach a compromise on the religious issues that divided Germany. In the meantime, Suleyman resumed his campaigns in the Danube valley. Charles felt that something had to be done about the Turkish menace, but knew that his exhausted subjects were unprepared to aid the beleaguered Ferdinand. The Spanish and the Italians, however, might be persuaded to pay for an attack on Algiers. His preparations began in earnest only after the collapse of the Diet of Regensburg in July. Naples contributed 202 000 ducats, Sicily 30 000, and Castile 150 000 in addition to the 180 000 already committed on an annual basis to the naval contractors Andrea Doria and Bernardino de Mendoza. An invasion fleet was assembled, but by this time it was October. Though his military advisors argued that it was foolhardy to attempt a landing on a lee shore at the beginning of the autumn storms, Charles felt that his credibility was at stake and would not be deterrred. On 21 October the Emperor and his men landed and began the investment of Algiers. The next day, a storm from the north drove 150 of his ships ashore. In the face of appalling losses in men and supplies Charles decided to re-embark, and the remnants of his army sailed for home in the few overcrowded vessels that had survived.

The disaster at Algiers marked the end of imperial designs in North Africa and left the Barbary pirates free to resume their depredations. It encouraged the French to resume hostilities in 1542 and brought the Turkish fleet, at least temporarily, into the western Mediterranean. From 1542 to 1544, Charles was preoccupied with the French war. After that, his attentions turned to Germany. In 1546 Barbarossa, now over 80, died in bed. His place was taken by the equally formidable Turgut Re'is (Dragut) who survived an attack by Andrea Doria in 1550 and seized Tripoli in 1551. The Spanish *presidios* in North Africa dwindled to two, and for more than 200 years the North Africans continued to trouble the coasts of Spain and Italy while interfering sporadically with the ships of other nations.

The Emperor failed to contain the Muslim threat in the Mediterranean because he could not seize and retain the North African ports. To do so would have required control over the rural areas of the Maghrib, and this was out of the question. The pirate regencies were Muslim and had the advantage of Turkish help, but even they could preserve order in the hinterlands only with great difficulty. Resistance to a Christian power would have been total. As an alternative, Cardinal Juan Pardo de Tavera, Archbishop of Toledo and erstwhile President of the Council of Castile, had long advocated controlling the sea with a permanent fleet specifically constructed and trained for that purpose, but this, too, was clearly beyond the Emperor's resources. Given the extent of his commitments, Charles had no choice but to pursue a policy that was at best opportunistic. He could deal with the North Africans only on occasion and could offer no long-term assistance whatever to his brother Ferdinand. It might be argued that his efforts, though sporadic, slowed the Ottoman advance, but this is doubtful. Logistics limited Turkish expansion in Europe. In the Mediterranean, the pirates had neither the desire nor the ability to extend their sovereignty beyond the towns of the Maghrib. They sought to loot, and loot they did. To Charles, who liked to see himself as the defender of Christendom, his performance against the infidel was one of the greatest of his many disappointments.

THE GERMAN PROBLEM

In terms of his own policies and desires, the Emperor's failure to resolve the problem of Germany on his own terms was even more disturbing than his failure to defeat the Turks. It was also far more important to the future of Europe. Charles believed in the old religion and in the ideal of imperial unity. Though capable of compromise in the short term, he saw the two as inseparable and tended to judge the success of his reign in terms of their preservation. The growth of princely autonomy and the religious Reformation that nourished it therefore struck at the core of his policy. From the beginning of his reign he saw both movements as mortal threats, but could do little to contain either.

The teachings of Luther and a growing host of other reformers gained ground steadily after the Diet of Worms, both among princes and among the citizens of the imperial towns. Even those city councils whose natural conservatism predisposed them against religious change found themselves under terrible pressure to break with the Old Church. Others openly embraced reform. Some townspeople supported the message of the reformers because they thought they understood it and believed that it offered a truer interpretation of the Gospels than that provided by the traditions of the Old Church. Some merely resented the established religious order. They felt that the privileges and immunities of the Church ran counter to their ideal of communal responsibility and knew that the confiscation and sale of Church properties could add greatly to the city's wealth both now and in the future. Princely motives were equally complex. Several rulers, including the young Philip, Landgrave of Hesse, were genuinely drawn to the new doctrines. Others took a proprietary pride in 'their' churches and resented what they saw as papal interference. Above all, princes knew that by breaking with the Church they could increase their revenues, strengthen their reserves of patronage, and gain control of an important complex of religious, educational, and charitable institutions without alienating their subjects. Given their universal desire for increased power and autonomy, it is perhaps surprising that any of the secular princes remained Catholic. Of those who did, many, like Charles himself, were attached by conviction to the Old Church. Some wished to remain on good terms with the Habsburgs or could not bear the thought of making common cause with a hated neighbor who had turned Protestant. Whatever their motives, Catholics retained a majority in both the Imperial Diet and the electoral college throughout the reign. Though never fail-safe and always dependent upon the bishops, this majority remained one of the few really effective weapons in the Emperor's German arsenal.

At the same time, the social unrest that had been building in Germany for nearly a century boiled over in a series of revolts whose connection with religion, though sometimes tenuous, was reinforced by the sixteenth-century tendency to use religious language in dealing with social and economic issues. One source of trouble was the imperial knights, who lacked political representation and whose economic position had been eroding for years. They found a leader in the mercenary contractor, Franz von Sickingen, who in 1522–23 launched an attack on ecclesiastical properties in the name of reform. A coalition of princes, some of whom were themselves on the edge of conversion, crushed the revolt. Sickingen perished in a cellar. A year later, in 1524, the long tradition of the *Bundschuh* revolts found ultimate expression in the Great Peasant's War. Once again, a coalition of princes defeated peasant armies that were often poorly armed and badly led.

Throughout all this the Emperor was absent in Spain, struggling with the aftermath of the *comunero* revolt. Though he personally had little to do with the Peasant's War, its consequences remain an important legacy of his reign. Among them was an increase in the power and self-consciousness of the princes. They, not he, had ended a mortal threat to their interests and to their conception of the Empire. They had proved to themselves that they could form effective coalitions and stand on their own in a moment of crisis. It is not surprising, then, that as the religious issue grew more heated the princes on both sides grew more assertive and less willing to compromise. The growing confidence of those who favored reform became apparent as early as the Diet of Nuremberg in 1524. They rejected a papal–imperial demand to implement the sentence pronounced against Luther at Worms because, in a moment of candor, Pope Adrian had admitted that the papacy was partially at fault for the abuses he had condemned. In 1526 at the Diet of Speyer they demanded a national meeting to discuss religious issues, arguing that until such a meeting took place, each prince and each city had the right to adopt its own religious policies.

Those policies became more diverse as new interpretations of reformed doctrine emerged. Luther, Zwingli, and other reformers disagreed over a number of issues, the most serious of which was the nature of the sacraments, especially the Eucharist. By 1529 the Reformation was itself fragmented, but several princes, and many cities had broken openly with the Old Church and tension within the Empire had reached new heights. In 1528 a dubious character named Otto von Pack forged a letter claiming that the Catholics were forming a hostile alliance. The young Landgrave Philip of Hesse, backed diplomatically by the Elector of Saxony, the King of Denmark, and the Voivod of Transylvania, responded by invading the bishoprics of Mainz and Würzberg. The crisis ended when the forgery was exposed, but at the Diet of Speyer in 1529 Archduke Ferdinand chose to reignite the embers of controversy. The Emperor, more cautious than his brother, sent instructions that he intended to be conciliatory. When their arrival was delayed, Ferdinand issued his own statement. He condemned the idea that each state could determine its own religion, demanded tolerance for Catholics throughout the Empire, and threatened to destroy the Anabaptists and Zwinglians. A majority of the delegates agreed to support this position, but on 19 April, 1529, the Elector of Saxony, Philip of Hesse, several other princes, and the representatives of 16 imperial cities signed a Protestation against the majority view. The signatories were thereafter called Protestants. Three days later, Hesse, Electoral Saxony, and the cities of Ulm, Strassburg, and Nuremberg formed a defensive alliance to protect themselves against the Catholics.

The more farsighted of the Protestants, led by Philip of Hesse, saw that this was not enough. They feared that doctrinal disputes might ultimately erode their united front against Catholicism and in October, 1529, Philip convened a colloquy of the leading reformed theologians at Marburg, hoping that they could arrive at a statement of common beliefs. Surprisingly, they almost succeeded. The Marburg Colloquy was conducted in an atmosphere of brotherly cooperation, and though the delegates continued to disagree on the vital issue of the sacraments, they parted without an open rupture. That was reserved for a second meeting, this time of the politicians, at Schmalkalden. Citing irreconcilable differences in sacramental theology, Nuremburg, Anhalt, and Electoral Saxony refused to join the others in making a common representation to the Emperor.

When Charles returned to Germany in June, 1530, to open the Diet of Augsburg, he therefore hoped that a peaceful resolution of the German question could be arranged. There would be a clear majority of Catholic delegates and the Protestants were divided. He did not know it, but the Diet was already beginning to spiral out of control. In March, the German bishops had commissioned Dr Johan Eck, a professor of law at Ingolstadt famed as an opponent of Luther, to draw up no fewer than 404 articles stating the uncompromising position of the Catholics. Eck handed it to Charles shortly after the latter's arrival. The Elector of Saxony quickly arranged a response. His subject Philip Melanchthon, a colleague of Luther's at the University of Wittenberg and a formidable theologian in his own right, drew up what became the Augsburg Confession. This concise statement of what could now be called a Lutheran position was signed by Nuremburg, Reutlingen, and the leading Protestant princes and presented to Charles on 25 June. Still hoping for peace, Charles prevailed upon the Catholic delegates to endorse a moderate *Confutation*, but Melanchthon responded with an *Apologia* whose language was if anything less conciliatory than that of the Confession. There would be no doctrinal compromise at Augsburg.

Neither side, however, wanted war. Charles had long suspected that nothing less than a council of the entire Church would be needed to resolve the schism. He now wrote personally to the Pope, setting out the argument for a general council in great detail, but Clement VII refused to consider it. He feared, like other popes before and since, that a council could only weaken papal authority and make matters worse. Though Charles did not know it at the time of his proposal, the German princes would in any case have refused to attend. Their demand was for a general council of the German nation. The Diet of Augsburg ended in November with a recess or provisional document that embodied the most extreme Catholic positions and in effect outlawed those of the Protestants. Charles was himself out of patience with the reformers and for a time considered the possibility of war.

As the Emperor knew, the terms of the Augsburg recess could have been imposed only by force, but in fact nothing happened. More than 15 years would pass before the two sides took arms against each other. This was only in part because Charles remained distracted by France and the Turks. The Catholic princes, though they antagonized the Protestants at every turn, had no desire to fight them and by so doing enhance the power of the Habsburgs. They knew, too, that Charles was short of money after the Italian war of 1527–29 and lacked a significant force of his own in Germany. If war broke out they, not he, would bear its burden. Moreover, would not a quarrel among princes encourage another peasant revolt? They made their views clear as the Diet of Augsburg recessed. By this time the Habsburgs themselves had decided that hostilities should be avoided until the Archduke Ferdinand could be elected King of the Romans. The election was vital to their interests because it meant that Ferdinand would succeed Charles as Emperor if he survived his older brother. In the meantime it would enhance the Archduke's constitutional authority and strengthen his hand in governing the Empire as Charles's Regent.

The election was held at Cologne in January, 1531. All of the Electors present were Catholic and voted for Ferdinand, thanks in part to the 360 000 florins he had borrowed from the Fuggers to encourage them.

The Elector of Saxony refused to attend. He claimed that the election was invalid, as did the Bavarian Wittelsbachs, perhaps the most powerful of the Catholic princes. Following the anti-Habsburg traditions of their house, they not only opposed Ferdinand's election but in October, 1531, allied themselves with the Protestants without abandoning their support for the Old Church or modifying their anti-Protestant rhetoric. The election of Ferdinand, then, revealed divisions and uncertainties among the Catholics and made their cause appear weaker than it may actually have been. At the same time, it encouraged the Protestants to put aside their differences in the interest of self-preservation. They perceived the Emperor's exasperation at Augsburg as implacable hostility and saw Ferdinand's election as a tightening of the Habsburg noose. In February, 1531, six weeks after Ferdinand's coronation, Elector John of Saxony, Philip of Hesse, the Count of Mansfeld, Philip of Grubenhagen, the Dukes of Lüneburg, the Prince of Anhalt, and the cities of Strassburg, Ulm, Bremen, Magdeburg, Reutlingen, Memmingen, Constance, Isny, Biberach, and Lindau signed the *Compact* that formed the Schmalkaldic League. Like all leagues of independent states, that of Schmalkalden would be hampered by internal divisions and by failures of coordination, but its formation was nevertheless a development of the utmost significance. Based on the explicit assumption that princes and cities alike had the right to defend their subjects against imperial power, it evolved into what might have become an alternative constitutional order for the German Empire.[7] In the end it could not do so, but at a vital juncture in imperial history it gave the Protestant states a rudimentary structure for making common decisions and a defensive alliance capable of intimidating, though not defeating, a divided opposition.

After the formation of the Schmalkaldic League the Protestant cause grew stronger. Four of the Hanseatic towns converted by the end of 1531. In 1533 the Bavarians joined Philip of Hesse in restoring Württemburg to Duke Ulrich. The forces involved were paid largely by the French. Though keenly aware of the Duchy's strategic value to Habsburg lands in the southwest, Ferdinand did nothing. The defense of Vienna in 1532 had depleted his resources. Charles still lacked an effective military presence in Germany, and, in his own mind at least, Ferdinand's title as King of the Romans remained insecure. The Protestant princes had followed the lead of Saxony in refusing to recognize his election. Constitutionally, their refusal meant little, but Ferdinand wanted nothing to jeopardize his succession in an uncertain future. In 1534 he agreed to recognize the loss of Württemburg in return for their endorsement.

Ulrich lost no time in expropriating Church lands and introducing Lutheran preachers. Pomerania and Mecklenburg followed in the same year, and in 1535 the Lutheran Joachim II became Elector of Brandenburg on the death of his Catholic father. Ducal Saxony, a stronghold of Catholicism under Duke George, accepted the Reformation under his son Henry.

An attempt to revive the Swabian League with Habsburg support failed. There were lawsuits in the Catholic-controlled *Reichskammergericht* against Protestants who expropriated Church lands, but the Emperor, preoccupied in 1535 with the attack on Tunis and in 1536–38 with another war against France, knew that a military response to the German problem was out of the question. He began to think in terms of conciliation. In 1537 he sent the imperial Vice-Chancellor, Matthias Held, on what he hoped would be a good-will mission to the Protestants. Instead, the officious and conceited Held exceeded his instructions and in 1538 organized a Catholic League in opposition to that of Schmalkalden. Charles appears to have had nothing to do with this initiative.[8] None of the electors and only two bishops joined because both sides still hoped for peace. In 1539 Johann von Weese, Archbishop of Lund, replaced the discredited Held as chief imperial negotiator and arranged the Frankfurt Agreement, by which Charles agreed not to proceed against the Protestants by force and suspended the trials in the *Reichskammergericht* for six months.

Hope for an agreement on religious issues grew even brighter in 1540. Pope Paul III, who had succeeded Clement VII in 1534, was committed to Church reform. Though in most respects a classic Renaissance pope, Paul began to attack the more extreme forms of clerical misbehavior. Against the advice of his cardinals he had called for a general council in 1536. Charles had supported such a council for several years because he believed that only a meeting of all parties could end the religious division in the Empire. His own faith, though deep, was simple and traditional. Heinz Schilling has called it 'pre-confessional.' He had no interest in theological argument and never understood the spiritual aspirations that lay behind the Reformation. Like everyone else, he could see that the clergy had to be reformed, but the subtleties of sacramental theology and the finer nuances of justification eluded him completely. It would therefore be many years before he abandoned all hope of doctrinal compromise. He had pressed Clement VII to call a council, but the wily Pope feared that such a body would follow the example of its fifteenth-century predecessors and use its conciliar authority to undermine his own. When Paul III overcame his own similar fears Charles was delighted, but the plan of 1536 died when the French opposed it and the Protestants insisted on a Council of the German Nation to be held only on German soil.

Efforts at reform, however, continued. When his proposal for a Council failed, the Pope established a commission to study abuses within the Church under the presidency of Cardinal Gasparo Contarini, a known advocate of change. Printers somehow obtained copies of the commission's report, a devastating catalogue of clerical misdeeds, and its conclusions became a mainstay of Lutheran propaganda. Disastrous as these initiatives may have seemed, they demonstrated that the Holy See was at last willing to address the problems confronting it. Optimists on both sides began to hope for the reunification of Christendom. A series of talks among Protestant theologians at Hagenau in 1540 and then a discussion at Worms between Protestants and Catholics seemed to hold the promise of doctrinal compromise. Charles, who had encouraged these talks, once again began to hope for a way out of his German difficulties. He ordered the Colloquy between Catholics and Protestants moved to Regensburg in preparation for the Diet of 1541. Secret communications with Philip of Hesse encouraged his cautious, but growing optimism. The Landgrave Philip, an unconventional thinker in religion and politics, had contrived an original solution to his domestic problems as well. Like Henry VIII before him, Philip had grown disatisfied with his wife, Christina of Saxony, and wanted to marry another. After consulting Luther, Philip had followed the bigamous example of the patriarchs by taking a second wife. The resulting scandal did incalculable damage to Luther's reputation and to Protestantism as a whole while leaving Philip exposed to capital charges under imperial law. Fearing that even his horrified allies would turn against him, he drew closer to the Emperor and offered not only to obstruct Protestant relations with the French, but to assist Charles at the forthcoming Diet.

In the end, of course, both the Colloquy and the Diet of Regensburg failed. Melanchthon, Bucer of Strassburg, and the Hessian preacher Pistorius represented the Protestants. Gropper, Pflug, and the normally belligerent Eck negotiated for the Catholics under the daily supervision of Contarini. The learned and gentle Contarini was himself an optimist whose own views on justification would later appear semi-heretical. Melanchthon and Bucer were men of good will who genuinely deplored schism. Together they reached an agreement of sorts on the key issue of justification, but remained deadlocked on the sacraments and papal authority. They had nevertheless gone too far. Though Charles endorsed it as a basis for discussion, both Luther and the Pope repudiated the Colloquy's statement on justification. By July, both sides had rejected any agreement. Charles was now desperate to be gone. His brother Ferdinand needed immediate help against the Turks who had again invaded Hungary, and Charles had formed the notion of attacking Algiers. Though he concluded a treaty with Philip of Hesse in which the Landgrave agreed, incredibly, to support Charles against the Protestants, the Diet itself ended in acrimony.

The Diet of Regensburg marked a turning point in Charles's policy. He had considered force in 1530 but rejected it, and for more than a decade had followed a policy based on the hope of compromise. That he should have done so might appear remarkable, given his ardent attachment to the Old Church, but reconciliation did not appear as impossible then as it does in hindsight. Men of good will on both sides, Erasmus, Contarini, and Melanchthon among them, felt that the doctrinal issues might be resolved. Extremists, or perhaps those with a more rigorous sense of logic, doubted this, but the doctrinal issues were in themselves secondary. By 1541 they masked a growing chasm between the two faiths, not only in belief, but in everyday practice. There are Catholic theologians today who recognize that Luther was a theologian within the Catholic tradition, but the Reformation, like Luther's thought, had a momentum of its own. As Charles moved resolutely to disaster at Algiers, he must have realized that Protestantism involved a concept of religious life that was wholly unlike his own. Its adherents could neither be cajoled nor threatened, and their rulers would never willingly give up the material advantages provided by reform. The Emperor now knew that, sooner or later, he would have to restore imperial unity by force.

Action in Germany, however, had to be deferred. The campaign against Algiers and the French war of 1542–44, with its mortal threat to the safety of the Netherlands, absorbed all of the Emperor's energy and finances. After the Peace of Crépy freed him, or so he hoped, from the threat of French meddling in 1544, Charles turned again to the problems of Germany. The defeat of Duke William of Cleves ended any immediate threats to the Netherlands, but northwest Germany remained unstable. The strategic importance of this region was obvious both to the Habsburgs whose lands bordered it on the west and to Philip of Hesse on the south and east. Philip's interest in the region was represented by his relative, Bishop Franz von Waldeck, who ruled the dioceses of Münster, Osnabrück, Paderborn, and Minden. The leading ally of the Habsburgs was Duke Henry of Brunswick, a staunch Catholic, but one whose territorial ambitions alarmed his neighbors. When Henry had tried to seize the towns of Brunswick and Goslar in 1542, the armies of the Schmalkaldic League intervened. Taking advantage of the Emperor's preoccupation with France and Cleves, Philip of Hesse (whose panic over his bigamous marriage had now passed) and the Elector John Frederick of Saxony occupied the Duke's territories and began the conversion of his subjects.

The League's success emboldened reformers and would-be-reformers throughout the region. Bishop Waldeck began to permit reformed preaching at Osnabrück. To the south, Herman van der Wied, the Archbishop of Cologne and an Elector of the Empire, accepted the Reformation in 1543 and began to secularize Church lands with the support of his representative assembly. Three years later, the Elector Palatine also joined the reformed camp. The spread of reform along the porous borders of the Netherlands concerned the Emperor, but the conversion of the two Electors was cause for serious alarm. With Cologne and the Palatinate added to Saxony and Brandenburg, the Protestants now had a four-to-three majority in the electoral college. As Philip of Hesse injudiciously remarked, this meant that if Charles and Ferdinand both died, the next Emperor might be a Lutheran. He would almost certainly not be a Habsburg.

The League's triumph in the northwest and the subsequent spread of reform now represented a mortal threat to the Emperor's dynasty as well as to his faith and his conception of the Empire. Compromise no longer seemed possible. Pope Paul III had at last succeeded in calling a general council of the Church at Trent in 1545. In compliance with one of the clauses of the peace of Crépy, Francis I at last withdrew his opposition and permitted his bishops to attend. Years before Charles would have welcomed such a development, but at this point it made his task more difficult. The Protestants, secure in their strength, would not attend, and the existence of a general council precluded their demands for a meeting of the Germans. Charles could no longer hold out the possibility of a negotiated settlement, and though he tried at first to move the delegates at Trent toward a policy of conciliation, it was not to be. Within weeks it became clear that the Pope, the Italians, and even his own Spanish delegation supported a reaffirmation of Catholic teachings that would specifically condemn the innovations of Luther and his fellows. At the same time, the Pope made it clear that he would support a war against the German Protestants with both men and money.

Charles met with Philip of Hesse at Speyer in March, 1546, but found him once again firmly attached to his allies in the League. No purpose could be served by further delay. Imperial diplomats, ably led by Nicholas Perrenot de Granvelle, began to sow dissent in the Protestant ranks while consolidating his master's influence with the Catholics. One prong of this diplomatic offensive involved the Wittelsbach Dukes of Bavaria who, though Catholic in religion, had so far refused to support the policies of the Emperor. Citing the recent conversion of the Palatine Elector to Protestantism, Charles promised the Palatinate to the Elector's cousin, William of Bavaria, in return for Bavarian support against the Schmalkaldic League. The Elector abandoned the League, but saved his new religion and the Palatinate. William's son Albert then married King Ferdinand's eldest daughter, Anna. The Bavarians, in turn, agreed to provide material asssistence and the use of their territories to the Emperor, though they refused to fight. It was the beginning of what would become a permanent Habsburg–Wittelsbach alliance.

Meanwhile, Granvelle secured the backing of two Protestants, Margrave Albert Alcibiades of Brandenburg-Culmbach and Maurice, Duke of Saxony. Alchoholic and chronically bankrupt, Margrave Albert was more *condottiere* than prince, a man whose army and considerable military skill were usually available to the highest bidder. Maurice of Saxony was more sophisticated, though equally cynical. Nominally a Lutheran and married to Agnes, the daughter of Philip of Hesse, Maurice never allowed religion to impede his quest for political advantage. As Duke of Saxony since 1541 he had grown deeply suspicious of his cousin, the Elector John Frederick. Maurice had therefore supported the Emperor against France and Cleves in the war of 1543, and Granvelle now told him that if he helped to defeat the Schmalkaldic League by invading electoral Saxony, he could replace John Frederick as Elector if the Emperor won. The dream of reuniting the Albertine and Ernestine branches of his family's patrimony while achieving the electoral honor proved difficult to resist. With Bavaria, ducal Saxony, and Margrave Albert in hand, Charles felt free to proceed. True to his word, the Pope granted him Church revenues from Spain and the Netherlands and a contingent of Italian troops. The Fuggers advanced him 500 000 ducats against future revenues, and troops were raised throughout the empire, including three Spanish *tercios* under the Duke of Alba and a contingent of 10 000 Netherlanders under the Count of Buren.

The League, too, was busy. Its leaders refused to attend another Diet at Regensburg in June and July, 1546. Charles used his leisure to

conduct an illicit affair that resulted in the birth of a son, Don Juan of
Austria, who would command the Christian fleet at the great naval battle
of Lepanto in 1571. The Protestants spent the summer raising an army
which, in size at least, was greater than the Emperor's. On 20 July,
Charles outlawed Philip of Hesse and John Frederick of Saxony for their
continued occupation of Brunswick. Religious issues were not mentioned.
Shortly thereafter, the army of the League, commanded by Schertlin
von Burtenbach, marched south to confront Charles. From the beginning the Protestant command suffered from division and uncertainty of
purpose. Schertlin was a professional, but found that his every decision
was questioned by Philip of Hesse or the Elector John Frederick. The
Leaguers nevertheless managed to delay the arrival of the papal troops
by cutting off the Fern pass through which they hoped to enter the
Danube valley, but they failed to seize Regensburg where Charles still
awaited his reinforcements. Charles himself regarded this as an error,
but it is hard to see how the city could have been taken without a lengthy
siege that would in any case have been compromised by the arrival of the
Italians and Buren's Netherlanders.[9] By September the reinforcements
had arrived and the two sides were evenly matched. Charles, advised by
Alba and opposed on this by the more hot-headed Buren, chose not to
risk a battle. Instead, the imperialists conducted a war of position along
the Upper Danube until December. As Alba had predicted, the League's
divided command and relative shortage of money took its toll. Their
mercenaries began to desert, and by Christmas the remainder of the
League's army headed for winter quarters. Charles, however, kept the
core of his army intact.[10]

It was well that he did so. Maurice of Saxony had waited to see how
matters went along the Upper Danube and did not honor his promise to
attack electoral Saxony until November when the League's failure had
become obvious. John Frederick, after he returned from Bavaria,
responded by invading Maurice's lands in both ducal Saxony and the
Bohemian province of Lower Lusatia. This broadening of the war
directly threatened the interests of Ferdinand who, as King of Bohemia,
had been struggling over a variety of issues with the Bohemian Diet. By
February the Saxon princes had achieved military stalemate, but the
Diet took advantage of John Frederick's invasion of Lusatia to threaten
rebellion on the Elector's behalf if Ferdinand did not grant them concessions. With the Saxon war in doubt and his brother's kingdom engulfed
in turmoil, Charles marched toward Saxony. On the morning of
Sunday, 24 April, 1547, he found the Elector's army on the eastern bank

of the Elbe near Mühlberg. Thinking the river impassable, John Frederick had taken no precautions against attack. After a leisurely breakfast he went to Church without bothering to draw his men up in formation. In the hours before dawn an imperial reconnaissance party located a stretch of water shallow enough to cross on foot. Charles and his men forded the river and surprised the Elector at prayer, routing his army and taking him prisoner on the Lochau heath after a cavalry pursuit.

Charles saw the battle of Mühlberg and the campaigns that led up to it as his greatest triumph. He commissioned Titian to paint a great equestrian portrait of him in commemoration, and for a time, it seemed as though a settlement of the German problem was at least possible, if not imminent. Wittenberg surrendered – without Luther, who had died the year before – and the Lutheran Maurice of Saxony claimed his reward from Charles by becoming Elector of Saxony as well as Duke. Philip himself, encouraged by his son-in-law Maurice, surrendered to the Emperor and was imprisoned together with the deposed Elector John Frederick. Unsupported by Philip of Hesse, the war in the north ground to a stalemate. Bremen and Magdeburg remained Protestant, but Charles removed the renegade Bishop of Cologne and restored the lost lands of Henry of Brunswick.

Maurice had gained the electoral dignity he coveted, but the imprisonment of Philip came as a surprise. Knowing that he was already regarded as a traitor to the Protestant cause and that he would now be accused of conniving at his father-in-law's arrest as well, Maurice protested violently but to no avail. Charles remained adamant. Meanwhile, in the south, the Duchy of Württemburg once again submitted to the Emperor. Beyond the Empire, the international front remained quiet. Francis I had died in 1546 and Henry VIII followed him within the year. Hungary was at peace after the conclusion of a new treaty with the Turks. When the Diet of Augsburg convened in 1547, it therefore appeared that Charles could at last impose a settlement favorable to his interests, but the meeting, like so many before it, ended with no more than another temporary agreement. For all its bright promise, Mühlberg, like so many of the Emperor's triumphs, in the end resolved nothing.

Try as he might the Emperor could not devise a program of imperial reform that would be acceptable to the princes, nor could he enforce his edicts in states that remained independent even in defeat. Charles began the 1547 Diet of Augsburg by floating an ingenious scheme for a league of all the states within the Empire. It would have its own parliamentary, judicial, and administrative institutions. Those of the Empire, he said, would be abolished. The princes, led by the Catholic Dukes of Bavaria, saw this as another attempt to erode their powers and would have none of it. He then tried, with somewhat greater success, to contain and, if possible, to reverse the religious progress of the Reformation. The Council of Trent had recessed in June, 1547, after showing little willingness to compromise with the reformers. Charles had no illusions about its speedy revival and therefore proposed the Augsburg Interim of 1548. As passed by the Catholic majority in the Diet, it restated Catholic doctrines and agreed to protect Catholics and Catholic practices in Protestant areas until such time as a revived Council of Trent might issue its final decrees. A number of the Protestants accepted the Interim because it made modest concessions on such issues as clerical marriage and justification while agreeing on the need for reform and permitting communion in two kinds.

Charles appears to have had great hopes for this agreement. If so, it is another sign that he misunderstood the nature of the Protestant threat. The Interim was partially successful only in those areas controlled or directly threatened by Charles's troops. Elsewhere, it was denounced or ignored. Towns with a Protestant majority continued to harass Catholics. Some of the princes who accepted the agreement did so reluctantly or with no intention of enforcing it. Philip of Hesse felt that as the Emperor's prisoner he had to endorse the Interim if he hoped to receive better treatment. The rulers of Württemburg, the Palatinate, and Brandenburg-Ansbach accepted the Interim because they hoped for imperial concessions on other matters, but did little or nothing to secure its enforcement. In all of these states Lutheran preachers continued to preach and administer the sacraments in the usual manner.

The Saxon Maurice skirted the issue by commissioning Melanchthon and Bishop Pflug of Naumburg to draw up a substitute document known as the Leipzig Interim. It restated Lutheran doctrines but allowed the use of Latin, the observance of Catholic feasts, and recognized the seven Catholic sacraments. Melanchthon referred to such matters as *adiaphora*, or theologically indifferent practices. His ecclesiastical colleagues disagreed. Anger at his compromise marked the beginning of a schism within Lutheranism that pitted Melanchthon's followers against the more rigorous Gnesio-Lutherans. The triumph of the latter, though not formalized until 1580, could have been foreseen in 1548–50. Saxony and the estates of Electoral Brandenburg accepted the Leipzig Interim, but most of the clergy in both countries failed to observe its provisions. The princes of north Germany and the cities of Hamburg, Bremen, and

Göttingen refused to accept either agreement, and Magdeburg became a center of vigorous Lutheran propaganda and resistance. If anything, the Augsburg Interim hardened Protestant sentiment and set the stage for disasters yet to come.

Thwarted once again in his attempt to impose order on the Empire, Charles returned to the vexed issue of his succession, and for the next three years was distracted by negotiations with his own family and other issues largely unrelated to German affairs. This inattention proved fatal to whatever was left of his German policy. Maurice of Saxony had been the chief beneficiary of the Schmalkaldic War. He now ruled both ducal and electoral Saxony and was besieging Magdeburg as the Emperor's surrogate, but to his clever, restless mind the situation was full of peril. The Protestants despised him for his evident betrayal of their cause and for his role in the capture of Philip of Hesse. By 1550, the princes of northeast Germany had organized themselves into a league at Königsberg. Led by John Albert of Mecklenburg, Duke Albert of Prussia and Margrave Hans of Küstrin, who had fought for Charles in the Schmalkaldic Wars but rejected the Augsburg Interim, they regarded Maurice as a more immediate enemy than the Emperor, and sought to relieve his siege of Magdeburg. The Catholics, too, distrusted him. They knew that the Interim was for all practical purposes a dead letter in both Saxonies and that Maurice's siege of Magdeburg had been deliberately unenthusiastic. They guessed that, though he hoped to become the city's 'protector' if it fell, his real motive in fighting was to prolong the siege while using imperial subsidies to build up his army for other purposes.

In fact Maurice's interests were not those of the Emperor. He was still angry over the imprisonment of his father-in-law, and saw the Emperor's enforcement of the Interim with 'Spanish' troops as an infringement of princely rights that he likened to slavery. Encouraged by Hans of Küstrin, whose dedication to the Lutheran cause was equalled by his cunning, Maurice began to explore contacts with his Protestant neighbors and, more ominously, with France. At this point, Charles might have allayed the Saxon's fears by releasing Philip of Hesse, but he refused to do so. Instead, he threatened to release the former Elector, John Frederick, when he learned that Maurice had been consorting with members of the League of Königsberg. The threat backfired. Faced with the possible loss of electoral Saxony, Maurice felt that he had no choice but to join the League himself at the beginning of 1551. A year later, at the same hunting lodge on the Lochau Heath where John Frederick had surrendered after the battle of Mühlberg, Maurice and the League expanded their alliance to include Henry II of France. France would provide financial support for a military campaign against the Emperor in return for the towns of Metz, Cambrai, Toul, and Verdun. Only Hans of Küstrin objected to this cession of imperial territory and left the League in protest. Henry confirmed the treaty at the end of January, 1552, and in March, Maurice's ally, the volatile Albert Alcibiades of Brandenburg-Kulmbach attacked Donauwörth. A French army under the Duke of Guise took Metz, Toul, and Verdun, and Maurice's own army, swollen with imperial subsidies intended for the capture of Magdeburg and supported by the mercenaries of the League, swarmed into Franconia and Swabia.

Charles was totally unprepared. With the succession issue settled, he had turned his attention to Italy where he hoped, after long delay and frustration, to incorporate the Duchy of Parma into Milan. The Parma question had become a symbol of his difficulties with the papacy and of his own shifting position on the Council of Trent. In 1545, the Emperor had allowed Paul III to grant Parma to his son, Pier Luigi Farnese, as part of his efforts to promote an alliance with the papacy. In 1550 a new Pope, the short-lived Julius III, had confirmed Pier Luigi's son, Ottavio, as Duke, but the situation had since changed. In the following year Julius decided to reconvene the Council of Trent, but Charles now objected. He knew that doctrinal compromise was impossible and that the Council would only exacerbate the situation in Germany by forcefully restating Catholic views. To secure his support, Julius offered to return Parma to Charles. Charles was happy to accept, and the terrified Ottavio Farnese turned to the French for protection.[11] In the spring of 1552, the imperial army was therefore in Italy trying to make good on the Emperor's new claim to Parma. Cut off from the Netherlands by Maurice's army and protected by little more than a bodyguard, Charles fled ignominiously to Innsbruck and then to Villach, where he sought refuge with his brother Ferdinand.

As Maurice himself anticipated, the Emperor's humiliation proved temporary. His army quickly returned from Italy and was joined by a contingent from Spain commanded by Alba. The always flexible Maurice renounced the French alliance before the troops arrived, and by enlisting the good offices of Archduke Ferdinand, began the talks that would lead by year's end to the Peace of Passau. Though technically no more than a truce, Passau was important. Charles released John Frederick of Saxony and Philip of Hesse, and for the first time admitted Protestants to the *Reichskammergericht*. He did not, however, formally recognize Protestantism or revoke the Interim, though the agreement delayed its implementation until more permanent arrangements could be made at the next Diet. Charles, his army now swollen to more than 60 000 men, marched off to besiege Metz in the snows of November. As at Algiers, he chose to ignore the advice of his military men, and once again temerity resulted in failure. The French garrison held, and by Christmas his force, tormented by cold and disease, withdrew. Metz would be the last campaign of his career.

3

FINANCING THE EMPIRE

Among the many legacies of Charles V was the crushing burden of debt that he left to his son and, more importantly, to the people of his many realms. That debt was incurred overwhelmingly by war. Charles was not personally extravagant. He dressed simply and built little, in part because his itinerant mode of life made the construction of palaces irrelevant. He once told his son that 'kings do not need to have residences,'[1] a bit of advice that Philip II conspicuously ignored. Constant movement, however, was expensive. A major journey requiring ships and a military escort might cost as much as a small campaign. Charles also spent grandly on the gifts, bribes, and favors that were expected not only by his loyal servants but by the diplomatic conventions of the age. Like his contemporaries, Francis I and Henry VIII, he knew that a certain magnificence was essential to his reputation. Yet when all this is added to the costs imposed by his notorious fondness for women and rich foods, the expenses of his Court rarely amounted to more than a modest fraction of the imperial budget, about 200 000 ducats in a typical year. Spending on all other non-military expenses (administrative, judicial, etc.) in each of his realms was proportionately even smaller. The total salaries of all of his Spanish councillors, judges, and treasury officials, for example, averaged less than 38 000 ducats per year. Local officials (*alcaldes, corregidores,* etc.) consumed another 4300 ducats, while embassies and diplomatic missions averaged between 50 000 and 60 000.[2] By contrast, in many of the years of his reign, war alone consumed more than the revenues available from his various states combined.

Charles made up the deficit by borrowing. In this he was no different from other princes; Francis I and Henry VIII did likewise with similar results. Yet it was not merely the amounts borrowed by sixteenth-century monarchs, but the ways in which they borrowed them that caused infinite difficulties for taxpayers and creditors alike. As Richard Ehrenberg noted long ago, the financial mechanisms of the day were inadequate to the burdens placed upon them by the growing cost of war. At the beginning of the reign the practice of funding debt with bonds, though known since the thirteenth century, was relatively uncommon outside Italy, and the bourses at Antwerp and Lyon were as yet poorly developed.[3] Moreover, rulers still tended to think of the lands they ruled as their personal property rather than as a public trust. Neither Charles nor any of his contemporaries recoiled at the idea of stripping assets or mortgaging future revenues on the basis of their word alone, and though they knew that their revenues were a renewable asset, they were far more concerned with the demands of war and the need to maintain a reputation than with careful fiscal management.

The finances of Charles V are well documented. Sources of revenue and credit have been carefully studied by Ramón Carande and others, but a study of the Emperor's financial position as a whole presents certain difficulties. There was, to begin with, no system for allocating expenses and contributions among the various realms. No one seems to have thought of such a thing, but if they had, they would have been well-advised to keep quiet about it. A greater incitement to political strife among Charles's territories would be hard to imagine. Funds drawn by Charles as Emperor came from all of his different realms in varying amounts and were co-mingled after receipt, which makes it difficult to relate expenditures to a specific revenue source or to determine the relative contribution of his kingdoms over time. The argument between his Netherlandish and Spanish subjects over who had contributed most rages to this day.

Moreover, any attempt to analyze expenditures as a whole is complicated by the fact that payments were made not only from imperial funds, but from accounts in each of the Emperor's different realms. Garrisons, fortifications, and the cost of galley contracts for naval defense were normally paid for from the revenues of the realms in which they were incurred. In the Netherlands money raised by cities and provinces from excises and other taxes was often spent directly on mercenaries or naval expeditions sponsored by the provinces. Funds derived from extraordinary *aides* usually went, not to the Emperor, but to the Regent's government which raised the armies and appointed the commanders who defended the country against the French. The Emperor and his Court usually had little or nothing to do with any of this.

Representative bodies in all of the realms bitterly opposed the allocation of money outside the country in which it was raised. Spain and the kingdom of Naples produced a surplus beyond what was needed for their own defense and therefore found it impossible to avoid subsidizing the Emperor's projects in places like Germany, about which they cared little. They tried, like their counterparts in the Netherlands, to influence how the money was spent, but in emergencies money tended to be drawn from those accounts which showed a positive balance with little regard for their original or stated purpose. Many of these accounts therefore contain items whose purpose is unclear. A grant or Court appointment made to an individual from the household account of the Regent Mary in the Netherlands might, for example, be a reward for military service in Italy by commanders of Netherlandish origin such as Lannoy or Philibert of Orange. Confusion over the true purposes of an expenditure can be resolved only through supporting documentation, if it is available. Attempts to reconstruct an individual set of transactions in detail can therefore require detective work of a high order, but the broad outlines of imperial finance as it evolved during the reign are relatively clear.

Because most of his reign was spent in continuous warfare on several fronts, Charles almost always spent more than he raised from taxes and his personal domain revenues combined. When his expenses, or those of any other sixteenth-century prince, exceeded annual revenues plus cash in hand, he had several alternatives. One was to sell Crown lands either to individual investors or to peasant cultivators who hoped to incorporate their villages as towns. Other assets available for sale included civil and judicial offices, military commissions, and monopolies. The great advantage of such sales was that they were more popular than taxes, but rulers saw this kind of asset stripping only as a necessary evil. Land sales permanently alienated parts of the royal domain, though in some cases peasants could be forced by legal maneuvering to buy their privileges more than once. Offices, however, were a renewable resource as long as the prince did not make them hereditary. Selling them did little to ensure administrative or military competence, but conscientious rulers tried with varying degrees of success to screen applicants for ability as well as deep pockets.

Borrowing offered the only real alternative to such practices. Forced loans had been common in the Middle Ages as had loans from bankers in which land, the Crown jewels, and other tangible assets were offered as collateral. These methods were still used, though their importance had already begun to recede in the fifteenth century. Money could also be borrowed against anticipated revenue, a relatively modern practice that became universal in the age of Charles V. Bankers loaned large sums in return for the proceeds of a specific tax or other source, payable at a date and time specified in the loan agreement or *asiento*. The borrowed money could then be sent in the form of negotiable bills of exchange directly to an army paymaster or other official anywhere in Europe. The speed and efficiency of the system was vital in an age when unpaid troops often disrupted campaigns by mass desertion or mutiny.

Under Charles V, loans of this kind were normally to be repaid in Antwerp at one of the quarterly fairs, though Genoa and Medina del Campo were often used as well. At traditional fairs merchants actually gathered to exchange merchandise, but Antwerp had by this time developed a permanent exchange or bourse. Its fairs were now little more than traditional dates for the settling of payments. French government loans were usually contracted and paid at Lyons. In some cases agents of the bankers themselves collected the taxes on which the loans were secured, a provision that further weakened the government's already shaky control of its finances. The interest paid on these loans was typically between 12 percent and 20 percent. This was high in an age when ecclesiastical authorities regarded anything above 5 percent as usury, but lenders knew that their chances of being paid on time were slim.

Costs in wartime are rarely containable. Wars tend to generate successive emergencies that prevent the timely payment of existing loans and demand further borrowing. Moreover, if a sovereign prince repudiated his debts, there was little his creditors could do about it beyond denying him further credit. If they were the prince's subjects, they might not even be able to do that, for princes possessed the means to extort loans from those who wished to do business in their kingdoms. Interest rates reflected these uncertainties, and princes were normally regarded as poor risks. In a further effort to protect themselves, lenders imposed supplementary charges if payment was not made on time. These 'handling charges' were based on a percentage of the loan's basic rate, and like the basic rate, varied according to the the ruler's credit and current political situation. After his victory at Mühlberg (1547), for example, Charles had to pay charges of only 14 percent; after the disaster at Metz (1552), the rate rose to nearly 100 percent. In time, the accumulated interest and charges on a given loan could easily exceed the value of the principle. These loans, whose principle could remain unpaid for decades while handling charges accumulated, are conventionally known as 'floating' debt.

Funded debt, or bonds – called *renten* in Dutch and *juros* in Spanish – carried lower payments, typically from 4 percent to 10 percent, but did not become an important financial tool until the 1540s. Unlike the floating debt based on *asientos*, bonds are not only pledged against specific revenues, but offer guaranteed payments at fixed intervals. Beginning in the reign of Charles V, they could be bought and sold openly at market rates on European bourses. Then, as now, price was determined by their relative safety and by interest fluctuations in the broader market. Bonds of this kind were rarely issued directly by the prince, but by a city or province whose credit was invariably better than his. Even the 'Court Bonds' issued by the imperial Court and bearing the personal endorsement of the Emperor usually had to be guaranteed by some high Court official or by a city whose credit was unassailable. The wise banker preferred to have a creditworthy intermediary between himself and the Crown. The system of funded debt reached its highest level of sophistication in the Netherlands. Provinces issued bonds on the Emperor's behalf against *aides* that had been voted, but not yet collected. Investors also favored municipal bonds that were normally funded by the excise taxes paid on everyday commodities. In both cases, the proceeds might go to the imperial treasury, but the obligation to repay rested with the city council or the provincial States. Small investors wishing to buy such bonds had to do so through the mediation of large bankers, who bought them in bulk and issued declarations of trust to their depositors on their own behalf.

By its very nature the funded debt would create few problems for Charles and his successors. The floating debt, on the other hand, soon reached intolerable proportions. In the course of his reign, Charles borrowed no less than 29 million ducats by *asiento* in Spain alone, with a repayment obligation of 38 million including interest and charges. His total revenues are almost as difficult to calculate as his expenses, but great as they were, they could not cover or even service debts of this magnitude. From 1520 to 1530, his proceeds from the Netherlands rose from 500 000 ducats per annum to 750 000. By 1544 they had reached 2.5 million and by 1555, 3.25 million per annum. The Castilian *alcabala* produced about 1.25 million ducats annually throughout the reign. *Servicios* voted by the Cortes rose steadily from 130 000 ducats in 1524 to 470 000 in 1555, and the King's share of bullion from the New World brought in 6.25 million ducats between 1546 and 1555, though the amounts varied widely from year to year and were almost wholly unpredictable.

Charles also received large contributions from the Church in Castile, including the *cruzada*, or crusade tax, the *tercios reales*, amounting to one-third of all tithes, and a *subsidio* voted by the clergy of all of his Spanish kingdoms at regular intervals and based upon a percentage of clerical incomes. Spanish taxes, however, increased by only 50 percent in the course of the reign, a rate far slower than that of tax increases in the Netherlands and barely greater than the rate of inflation, which in Spain averaged an estimated 2.8 percent throughout the reign. The *parlementum* of Naples voted a total of 8 million ducats in *donativi* during the reign, including the extraordinary grant of 800 000 ducats that helped save the Emperor in the debâcle of 1552. Lesser sums came from Aragon (100 000 ducats per annum) and Germany, where appropriations by the Imperial Diet tended to grow smaller with the passage of time. Overall, Germany seems to have contributed a total of no more than 4.5 million florins or about 3.2 million ducats in the 34 years between 1521 and 1555. There were also windfalls like the dowry of Isabella of Portugal, the ransom of Francis I's sons after Pavia, the bullion from Peru in 1535, and the 350 000 ducats received from the sale of the Moluccas to Portugal in 1529.

These figures, though very approximate, reveal that the Netherlands probably did contribute more to the imperial cause than any of the Emperor's other realms, yet Charles frequently said that it was upon Spain that he depended for financing. The reason for this paradox is that the exposed strategic position of the Netherlands ensured that most of the money raised there had to be used locally and was not available for use in Italy, Germany, or against the Turks. The situation is analagous to that of Milan, where taxes were if anything higher than in the Netherlands but consumed entirely by local defense. Moreover, because the cities and provinces of the Netherlands raised money whenever possible through the sale of bonds, they encumbered their revenues before the Emperor could use them as security for his *asientos*.

In comparison, the defense needs of Castile were relatively modest. The bulk of Spanish revenues were available for use elsewhere, and though the Spanish resorted to bonds (*juros*) with increasing frequency as the reign progressed, the funded debt remained small in comparison with that of the Low Countries. Most of the receipts from Castile and the Americas could therefore be pledged as security against the floating debt. This is why, by the end of the reign, the Spanish unfunded debt stood at 12 million ducats, four times that of the Netherlands. By controlling their own debt, the Netherlanders preserved their credit. By allowing the Emperor to control its debt, Castile ended in default within two years of his abdication. The road to the Spanish bankruptcy of 1557 was neither short nor straight. We have seen that the imperial election cost Charles 850 000 ducats. Of this, 543 000 came from the Fugger bank, 143 000 from their Augsburg neighbors the Welsers, and 165 000 from Genoese and Florentine sources. At the Diet of Worms Charles and his bankers renegotiated these loans, securing them against expected revenues from Castile and the Tyrol. The outbreak of war with France caused payment to be deferred, and the interest rate on floating loans rose to about 20 percent. To preserve his credit, Charles resorted to the sale of domain lands, some of which were purchased by his bankers. Such transactions were typical of the age. Investors in the debt of kings knew that repayment was at best uncertain. To keep them attached to his interests, Charles and his successors favored his bankers with inducements that had nothing – and everything – to do with the terms of their loans. In addition to selling his creditors land at favorable prices, he offered them honors, favors, privileges, and lucrative bits of business such as the galley contracts awarded to the Doria family of Genoa after 1528. The Doria were not only bankers, but maritime contractors. By paying them to maintain a fleet of galleys for the defense of the western Mediterranean, Charles not only increased their wealth, but made them his military partners.

Fortunately, French credit at this time was even worse than the Emperor's. After the victory at Pavia, caused in part by Francis's inability to pay his troops, Charles's credit grew better. Large loans had to be negotiated again during the war of 1527–29, but the bankers at first proved willing to meet his needs. As the costs of war escalated, credit grew tighter and the Ladies' Peace of 1529 owed more in the end to lack of money on both sides than to anything else. It was in this period that a fundamental change occurred in banking practices. Houses like the Fugger, who until then had made loans largely out of their own resources, now turned to borrowing money from smaller investors to raise the sums demanded.

The source of the Fugger's wealth, like that of the other Augsburg houses, had been commodities trading and the copper and silver from their mines in central Europe. In spite of problems with repayment, they had until about 1525 earned enormous sums from their imperial loans. The Augsburgers preferred whenever possible to make loans secured on

Austrian and German revenues because proximity and perhaps cultural considerations made them easier to collect. Charles assigned these assets to his brother in the 1520s, but Ferdinand, too, was an enthusiastic borrower, and the bankers continued to do well at his expense. The Fuggers are said to have averaged profits of more than 50 percent per annum during the early 1520s, but as the demand for credit rose, their own funds proved inadequate and they began to borrow money at the Antwerp bourse rate of 6–8 percent, to which they, as creditworthy bankers, were entitled. Relatively small investors became involved for the first time in imperial finance. To preserve their credit, the bankers had to repay these loans on time even if their own payments from the Crown were delayed. Their margins of profit therefore began to shrink, though the business as a whole remained profitable.

In the 1540s, as borrowing increased, funded debt became more important. The early years of the decade were a time of profound military crisis for the Low Countries. The war against France and Gelre forced city and provincial governments to impose new taxes and to issue a large number of bonds secured upon the expected returns. Each province adopted its own combination of taxes: excises, export duties, a tenth penny (10 percent) on commercial transactions, and even a tenth penny on annuities or profits from real estate. The most common, however, were excises on food, beer, and other commodities that fell most heavily upon the poor. Commercial interests blocked the export tax of 1541 in Holland, and though Flanders, Brabant, and Zeeland accepted a tenth penny in the crisis of 1543, they abolished it thereafter. To Netherlanders these were revolutionary *nieuwe middelen* (new expedients), not only because the taxes themselves were novel, but because they were perpetual and did not have to be voted upon at regular intervals like the *aides*.[4] Bolstered by these new revenues, the imperial government's receipts from the Netherlands increased threefold between 1540 and 1543.

The quality of bonds secured against these new revenues varied widely. Those guaranteed by the city of Antwerp or by the States of Brabant, for example, were accounted sound and retained favor with investors until long after the Spanish collapse of 1557. Those of the provincial Receivers General were issued largely on their own personal credit and often in quantities that exceeded the revenues available for their security. Investors distrusted them until the mid-1540s, when they became popular owing, it seems, to the efforts of Gaspar Ducci, the junkbond king of his day. For several years the bonds of the Receivers

General raised a great deal of money, but remained paper of dubious worth. Because the proceeds from this funded debt were spent almost entirely in the Netherlands by the government of Mary of Hungary, they had little effect on the number of *asientos* floated by the Emperor, which continued to grow as well. Increasingly, the new loans were secured against Spanish taxes, but there were other forms of collateral as well. Many of the loans needed to finance the Schmalkaldic Wars, for example, were secured against Pope Paul III's promise of a million ducats, much of which was to be raised by the sale of ecclesiastical lands in Castile.

The Emperor's credit may have improved after the victory at Mühlberg in 1547, but German bankers were becoming wary of a business in which the repayment of principle was so often delayed. Meanwhile, Spanish resentment grew as the proportion of money borrowed against Castilian revenues increased. That the money was being spent on matters of little interest to Spain was bad enough; that it was being collected by Germans was worse. Spanish officials began putting obstacles in the way of the bankers' agents and dragging their feet in general, or so it appeared. Anton Fugger, in particular, was finding it difficult to extract the money owed to him from Castile. He began to regret the close ties of his house with the Habsburgs and started to reduce his participation in imperial loans. Italians, and particularly the Genoese, gradually began to take the place of the Fuggers and Welsers as lenders of first resort, in part because the Spanish preferred to do business with them, and in part because the Italians were better placed geographically to profit from such related business as military contracting and the sale of Crown lands in Spain and Naples.

The Emperor's last years saw an unprecedented orgy of borrowing. The failed campaign for Metz alone cost more than 2.5 million ducats, and the wars that followed involved armies of unprecedented size and cost. Between 1552 and 1556 the government borrowed no less than 9 643 648 ducats in 121 *asientos* at an average interest rate of 48 percent including additional charges. Of this amount, nearly half was loaned by Italian bankers, about a quarter by the Germans, and the rest by bankers from Spain or the Netherlands.[5] Some of the loans were actually secured against existing Spanish *juros*, which is to say that the government was floating two or more loans on the same collateral. More new money was raised by reviving the unpopular confiscations of bullion from America. Royal officials took even the *bienes de difuntos* or goods of the dead, the hitherto sacrosanct property of those who had died in the Indies and whose often modest property was being distributed to their widows and orphans as an inheritance. The victims of this policy received government *juros* at a paltry 3 or 4 percent.

The willingness of otherwise sensible bankers to loan money in this highly speculative environment requires explanation. Some, of course, were drawn by interest rates beyond the dreams of avarice, but others advanced loans reluctantly and with great misgivings. During the 1550s relationships with the bankers were handled by the Emperor's secretary, Francisco de Eraso, the succcessor to Cobos who had died in 1547. Unlike the affable and subtle Cobos, Eraso was a bully; a hard man for hard times. He hectored reluctant investors, accusing them of being disloyal subjects and declaring outright what Cobos had preferred only to imply: that those who did not advance new monies would have to wait longer for the old. Then, after 1552, the Crown began to refuse export licenses to the great bankers, thereby forcing them to reinvest their profits in Castile. These tactics worked even on the Fuggers, who with great misgivings hastened to provide new funds on the principle of throwing good money after bad.

This state of affairs could not last. When Charles abdicated as King of Spain and ruler of the Netherlands, his son, Philip II, found that he could not meet the payments on the debt piled up by his father; retiring the principle was out of the question. In 1557 Castile declared what amounted to state bankruptcy by suspending payment on its debt. France quickly followed suit. Francis I in his declining years had at last learned the necessity of good credit. By curbing his expenditures and reorganizing his finances under the guidance of the able Cardinal de Tournon, he managed to leave a favorable situation for his son when he died in 1547. Henry II's resumption of the wars, however, soon placed him in a position like that of Charles V. In 1555 he negotiated *Le Grande Parti* which combined all existing floating loans with new ones equal to one-third of the old at 16 percent with a one percent sinking fund intended to retire the debt in ten years. The terms were far more favorable than those accorded Charles V in the same years, but it scarcely mattered. Three months after Philip II went into default, Henry followed.

The state bankruptcies of the sixteenth century did not involve Naples or the Netherlands, nor were they mere suspensions of payment. They converted floating debt to funded debt. In the case of Philip II, the government issued *juros* to the holders of *asientos* at much lower rates of interest, typically 6 or 7 percent. This not only reduced current charges, but put off the payment of principle indefinitely. Having restructured his inherited debts, Philip then proceeded to create more of his own. The final war with France that ended in 1559, his efforts to suppress the Revolt of the Netherlands, the ongoing struggle against the Turks, and the armadas against England were all funded primarily by *asiento*. Castilian revenues, including those from the New World, continued to increase, but they were never equal to the task of fighting on so many fronts. The Spanish Crown defaulted again in 1575, 1596, 1607, 1627, and 1647, yet lenders were always to be found until the very end.

The reasons for this optimism in the face of certain default are clear. Strange as it may seem, the business of loaning to the Spanish Crown remained profitable. In addition to the usual charges for late payment, bankers learned to incorporate a variety of brokerage charges and fictitious exchange rates into their loans, and to make even more money by timing the sale of bonds or bullion to their advantage at the fairs. Small investors in turn bought *juros* largely because they could find few other productive investments. Charles and his bankers had established a system for mismanaging finances that would last until the end of the Habsburg era.

The effect of these practices on the development of finance and of the European economy as a whole is hard to gauge. There can be little doubt that the age of Charles V marked a revolution in the development of financial markets and in the management of public debt. The emergence of funded government debt in the form of bonds issued on a large scale by Spain, the Netherlands, and France was in itself revolutionary. The development at Antwerp and Lyon of permanent exchanges on which those bonds and other securities could be traded at rates determined by the investors themselves marked an important stage in the evolution of the modern bourse. Financial practices, some of which are still in use, emerged amidst others that now seem arcane, inefficient, or even corrupt. The system itself remained fatally flawed, but it laid the ground-work for more successful measures in the future. On a less positive note, ruinous interest rates and the higher taxes needed to support them retarded economic growth. They may also have contributed to inflation-ary tendencies, especially in Spain, but there is no simple cause and effect relationship between the fiscal policies of Charles V and the eco-nomic development of his empire as a whole. Its component realms were too diverse to permit broad generalizations and must be dealt with individually.

4

THE ORDERING OF THE EMPIRE

The problem of financing the Emperor's wars affected each of his dominions in different ways. All, however, experienced profound economic and social change as the demands placed upon them by the Emperor's government increased under his successors. For this reason alone, the reign of Charles V marked a turning point in the history of the states he governed directly. But if war and paying for war consumed the best energies of the Emperor and his ministers, it did not cause them to neglect the day-to-day business of governance. Charles, like most of his contemporaries, saw it as his moral duty to maintain justice, preserve the faith, and provide an administration that was as efficient as war, poor communications, and meager resources permitted. Though he generally respected local institutions and did not consider himself a reformer, his governments made important changes in the administration of each of his states and in some cases created new structures where none had existed before.

Only a few of these reforms involved his empire as a whole. Among them was the establishment of a courier service that maintained communication among his various European realms. Early in the reign Charles granted the bulk of this business to Mafeo de Tasis of Bergamo, whose family continued to provide the Habsburgs with efficient mail service for more than a century. Distance, however, remained a formidable enemy. Relays of horse-mounted couriers could carry a message from Brussels to Valladolid in two weeks, but the journey normally required as much as a month. An army – or Charles's Court when travelling – rarely exceeded the speed of six to eight miles a day. Given the state of technology, little or nothing could be done about this beyond making

76

communications as safe and regular as possible. Charles and his government tried their best, but the implementation of policy was always beset with delays incomprehensible to the modern world.

Another reform created archives in each of the more important states and required that copies of all notarized documents in the Emperor's realms be preserved by notaries and surrendered to the government upon their retirement or death. Charles and his secretaries believed that an authoritative record of government decisions, legal proceedings, rights, and privileges would strengthen government and reduce disputes. The mass of historical data created by this policy has yet to be fully exploited by social and economic historians, but in its day it served as the documentary basis of both local and imperial administration. Most of the other changes introduced during the reign pertained only to the individual states whose political and economic development must therefore be considered on a regional basis.

THE SPANISH KINGDOMS

When Charles returned to Castile in the summer of 1522, the *comunero* revolt had been defeated, not by the Crown but by the efforts of the high nobility headed by the Admiral and Constable of Castile. The grievances of the towns remained, the treasury was depleted, and the young monarch lacked credibility even with the nobles who had intervened to save him. He responded to this daunting situation with a skill and delicacy that belied his youth.

His first challenge was to restore the monarchy's relationship with the towns. Charles knew that their complaints had been largely justified, but above all he needed their financial support and the future cooperation of local elites in the business of government. There would be no bloodbath and, by sixteenth-century standards at least, few reprisals. The general pardon sent to the towns before his arrival excluded only 293 of the most prominent rebel leaders. Of these, 23 were executed. Twenty more died in prison and the rest were pardoned in the next few years, often in return for a cash payment. At the same time, Charles revoked all grants and appointments made during his absence by the Admiral and Constable. Some he reestablished by royal *cédula*, but there would be no grants or *mercedes* for the nobles who had supported his cause. Even those who claimed damages at the hands of the *comuneros* would have to await the determination of special courts established by Charles. The *grandes*, led once again by Admiral Enríquez, protested, but the young King held firm. He knew that he had to reestablish his authority over the process of reconciliation before he could bring order to the realm as a whole and that, even had he wished to reward the nobles, his treasury was in no condition to support the kind of generosity they expected.

In fact the finances of Castile were in total disarray. For two years *comuneros* and supporters of the Crown alike had appropriated Crown revenues for their own use without notifying either of the chief financial departments of the state, the *hacienda* or the *contaduría mayor de cuentas*. The honesty and efficiency of both offices had long been compromised in any case. The *servicios* or extraordinary taxes voted by the Cortes in 1518 and 1520 had not been collected, and those of 1520–21 had been committed to foreign lenders who as yet remained unpaid. Castile owed the Fuggers alone more than 57 million *maravedís*, largely for the bribes paid to secure the imperial election. The French invasion of Navarre in 1521 added to the Crown's burdens. Though the treasurers Alonso Gutiérrez and Juan de Vozmediano confiscated the receipts of merchants from the Indies on their own authority (thereby suggesting an unfortunate precedent to the Crown), the government's creditors – and its soldiers – remained largely unpaid.

The obvious first step toward restoring confidence in the administration was to remove unpopular or corrupt officials. Gutiérrez and Vozmediano were replaced after an investigation into their affairs, as was the Viceroy of Navarre. The Royal Council had made itself unpopular during the revolt and Charles quickly replaced its President, Antonio de Rojas with Juan Pardo de Tavera, the Archbishop of Santiago. Tavera and the three new councillors appointed with him had played no part in suppressing the revolt and were therefore acceptable to the towns. By 1525 the King had also fired the presidents of both *audiencias* (the appellate courts at Valladolid and Granada) and replaced almost a dozen judges. Charles knew, however, that personnel changes were essentially cosmetic. If he hoped to govern effectively, he would have to change the system.

The reforms begun in 1522–25 expanded and transformed the government he had inherited from Ferdinand and Isabella without changing its basic character. In Castile, as in all of the Spanish and Italian kingdoms, Charles maintained the ancient tradition of household administration while adding new levels of complexity and sophistication. His first step was to create in 1522 a Council of Finance. Inspired by the Council of Finance in the Netherlands, it met daily to set fiscal policy and to supervise the various departments of the *hacienda* and the *contaduría mayor de cuentas*.

Under the guidance of Francisco de los Cobos, who remained its secretary until his death in 1546, it became a responsive instrument of imperial policy, often to the detriment of Castile itself. Cobos, a poor boy from the Andalusian town of Úbeda, had come up through one of the secretarial 'schools' that would remain a feature of the Castilian administration until the end of the Habsburg era. Royal secretaries took apprentices, trained them, and tried their best to place them in important positions, thereby creating important networks of patronage for themselves. In the course of the reign Cobos expanded his responsibilities until he became Charles's secretary for southern European affairs, the counterpart of Nicholas Perrenot de Granvelle in the north.

Cobos, like most of his fellows, never received a university education, but after 15 years of experience and careful observation he had learned the art of political navigation. Agreeable, shrewd, and by the standards of his time, honest, he saw himself purely as a facilitator of the King's will. Institutional loyalties of the kind that inspired the Imperial Chancellor Gattinara were to him irrelevant. If Charles needed money, Cobos would find it; if a royal policy were announced, he would find a way to implement it. In this he differed little from the other royal secretaries, a fact which helps to explain why these officials continued to grow in importance throughout the reign and beyond. From the perspective of the Crown, a system of councils whose agendas and final reports, or *consultas*, were drafted by loyal and efficient secretaries was almost perfect. It provided useful advice without in any way challenging the prerogatives of the King.

Charles used the same model in reforming the Royal Council itself, which had become as unwieldy as it was unpopular. As the only council that dealt with civil administration under Ferdinand and Isabella it had been forced to advise the Crown on all matters pertaining to the kingdom, including finance and the appointment of royal officials. In addition, like royal councils elsewhere, it served as a final court of appeal when other judicial remedies had been exhausted. By 1522 the case load accumulated during the years of turmoil promised to strangle its deliberations entirely. To Charles, the primary function of the council should have been administrative supervision and its highest calling the selection of honest and competent bureaucrats. Because he ruled other kingdoms as well, he renamed it the Council of Castile. To improve the efficiency of its deliberations, he reduced its membership from 16 to 8, while carefully limiting the number and types of judicial appeal that it was allowed to hear. This meant that the role and prestige of the *audiencias* would

have to be expanded, a process already begun with the replacement of
their presidents and many of the judges. By 1530 the *audiencias* had
become the final courts of appeal in cases involving aristocratic claims
arising from the revolt and the Crown's rights of patronage and pre-
sentation. They also dealt with a range of ecclesiastical issues that went
beyond patronage to include all conflicts over Church property and the
application of papal bulls within the kingdom.

The Council's primary function was now, as Charles had intended,
the vetting and appointment of Crown officials and the supervision of
visitas and *residencias*, the instruments through which the Crown had
always tried to ensure honesty and diligence in its officials. In this it differed from the Council of Aragon, whose portfolio remained largely as it
had been under Ferdinand. Aragon was, of course, smaller and its
finances less complicated than those of Castile. The Council of Aragon
would retain direct control over both the Chancellery and the Treasury,
though by custom the Treasurer of Aragon would always be a Castilian.
Neither of the royal councils was expected to provide advice on matters
of state. The Emperor, with his far-flung responsibilities, had no intention of allowing individual kingdoms to make policy without considering
imperial interests as a whole. For internal matters, Charles relied on the
advice of his secretaries. For imperial and international questions he
possessed a Council of State whose members were drawn from all of his
major possessions. It was largely honorific and rarely, if ever, met as a
body. The development of foreign and military policy was an informal
process in which Charles might, or might not, consult those members of
his itinerant Court who happened to be present at the time.

Everything, of course, depended upon the timely supply of money.
The Emperor knew that his imperial obligations would require frequent
servicios and other concessions from his Castilian subjects in addition to
the regular taxes over which they had no control. This meant that he
would have to restore his frayed relations with the Cortes and the urban
elites it represented. The keystone of his policy was to tie requests for
new taxes to a continuation of *encabezamiento*, the ancient system by
which city councils administered their own contributions to the royal
treasury. Of all the blunders committed by his government on the eve
of the *comunero* revolt, the proposal to abolish this system in favor of tax
farming had been among the worst. Now Charles embraced *encabezamiento*
with enthusiasm. City councils would negotiate their share of a new tax
with the government and collect it themselves as they had long done with
the *alcabala* and other levies. Each new request was accompanied by

a guarantee that the *encabezamiento* would be extended. Conversely, if a city's representatives failed to support a *servicio* in the Cortes, its government might be excluded from collecting it and left to the mercy of tax farmers retained by the Crown. To limit the discretion of individual members of the Cortes and to ensure that a city could not disavow the actions of their representatives, Charles eventually adopted the practice of asking each town council to vote publicly on the matter.

In this way the governing elites of the towns became partners with the King in the crucial business of administering taxes, a process facilitated by the latter's willingness to negotiate, often on the most personal of levels, for the city's vote. By 1525 Charles seems to have recognized that coercion was counterproductive. In the course of the reign he developed what amounted to a system of parliamentary management. Whenever a *servicio* was requested, he sent his personal representatives to meet with each town council. The representatives supported their arguments and inducements with personal letters from the Emperor addressed to individuals of importance and followed by equally personal letters of thanks when the measure passed. The process was not based solely on flattery. Cooperative leaders could expect tangible rewards, including salaried appointments and other honors. Charles's government was also more ready than its predecessors to redress grievances and approve legislation drafted by the assembly. Unlike Ferdinand and Isabella, who once went 18 years without a meeting of the Cortes, Charles averaged a meeting every three years. Though he never allowed petitions to be considered before the passage of revenue measures, he rarely ignored them. Nearly half of the legislative edicts produced during his reign proceeded in the first instance from petitions of the Cortes.

The only real failure experienced by Charles in his dealings with the Cortes occurred in 1538 when he asked that it impose a *sisa*, or excise tax, on food. Though regressive in the sense that it would fall most heavily upon poor people who spent the largest part of their incomes on food, the tax was nevertheless opposed by the rich. Castilian nobles had always been exempt from taxation. For this reason, they had rarely met as part of the Cortes. Thinking that an excise would be more acceptable if it were levied on everyone, Charles now asked the nobles to meet as an estate and support a tax that would apply equally to themselves. The nobles, of course, argued that the measure would end their traditional immunity from all taxation and refused. The commons followed suit and the measure failed. Never again would the nobles be invited to attend a meeting of the Cortes.

As in so many other areas of governance, Charles's policies were continued by his successors. The importance of the Cortes grew with time, but it never developed the truculent independence of the English Parliament. In line with the Emperor's careful planning, Castile's representative assembly instead became a central instrument of royal power that bound the cities and their governing classes ever more closely to the dynasty.[1] The policy of recruiting or co-opting the members of various elites would remain a central feature of the Habsburg system. Charles may have been suspicious of the *grandes*, as he proved in his celebrated instruction of 1543,[2] but if he never gave them everything they wanted, he remained careful of their dignity and generally supportive of their interests. They continued to receive lucrative appointments at Court, *mayorazgos* that permitted them to entail their estates, and even *mercedes* (outright gifts) in return for their support. Traditional rights over their *señorios*, or lordships, gave them a powerful role in local affairs, and the more competent among them held the highest military commands. Their complaints notwithstanding, titled aristocrats continued to be the most powerful element in the body politic after the Crown.

At the village level, Charles continued and expanded the ancient practice of selling municiple charters to village councils. His predecessors had done this, in part, by alienating municipal lands. They sold charters to those who had formerly owed dues and services to the royal towns, thereby offending the city governments and providing yet another grievance for the *comuneros*. Charles preferred to use the powers gained from a series of popes to alienate Church lands and those of the military orders. By so doing he extended his patronage to peasant elites and involved them in the work of rural government without offending either the nobles or the towns.[3] The Emperor never applied similar measures in Aragon, nor did he attempt to reform its administration or change the traditional – and rather prickly – relationship between Crown and Cortes. The most important reform of his reign in Aragon was the creation of a permanent committee of the Cortes to administer taxes between sessions. In Castile, however, he built upon foundations laid by his predecessors to create a state that, while formidably regalist in theory, involved a high degree of cooperation from his subjects.

The system of governance and administration by Charles V, though elaborated upon by his successors, remained intact for the remainder of the Habsburg period and helped make Castile one of the most stable kingdoms in Europe. That stability, and the steady supply of revenues that accompanied it, ensured that Castile would become in Charles's mind the indispensible core of his power, the realm upon which he could most rely in moments of crisis. Spanish military prowess reinforced that perception. Experience acquired in the wars against France reversed the decline of Spanish arms during the last years of Ferdinand of Aragon. In 1536 Charles reorganized an already effective fighting force into *tercios* with a nominal strength of 3000 pikemen and arquebusiers while retaining the basic tactical formulae developed in the days of Gonzalo de Córdoba. The *tercios*, though they rarely made up more than a third of an imperial army, served as its elite corps and would retain their dominance on the battlefields of Europe until the Thirty Years' War. The reforms of Charles V in Castile may have been incremental, but they laid the foundations of Spain's status as a great power in the century after his death.

In contrast, his fiscal policies established precedents that carried the virus of decline. Spain under Charles V enjoyed a period of demographic and economic growth that masked the effects of his financial irresponsibility. It was not until late in the reign of Philip II that the consequences of ruinous borrowing covered imperfectly by higher taxes became apparent. By then, economic decline had become irreversible.

Ironically, Castile was not the most heavily taxed of the Emperor's dominions. Castilian elites supported war against the Turk and understood that control of Italy best served their interests in the Mediterranean. They feared the French and were in a general way sympathetic to the struggle against German heretics, but there were limits to their compliance. Castilian taxes increased only 50 percent in the course of the reign, a rate far lower than the Crown's expenditures. The overall rate of taxation never approached that of the Netherlands, and scholars have argued that Castile, like Naples or Sicily, was not taxed to its capacity until early in the seventeenth century.[4] The problem was not taxation in itself, but the rate of borrowing, which built up monstrous debts that could only be funded by new taxes under Charles's successors. By the end of the century taxation had indeed reached ruinous levels.

The high interest rates paid on government loans may also have contributed to inflation. Jorge Nadal calculated that the rate of inflation in Castile averaged 2.8 percent per annum over the course of the reign, an astonishing figure for an agrarian economy before the industrial revolution. In 1934, Earl J. Hamilton adopted the monetarist argument that imports of bullion from the New World lowered the value of money by increasing the supply. His theory has since been questioned because much of the imported specie was shipped off immediately to pay for the

King's wars or for imports and could not have been absorbed by the Spanish economy. Some of it, however, remained, and Hamilton's thesis cannot be rejected in its entirety. A more serious problem, however, was population increase coupled with a growing demand for Spanish agricultural products in the New World. The colonists, as good Spaniards, would not accept a diet that lacked wine and oil. Grain lands in Andalusia gave way to vineyards and olive groves. The south began importing its grain from the north, but the peasants of La Mancha and Old Castile, already faced with increasing consumption in their own regions, found it difficult to meet the demand. Dry-land agriculture provides relatively inflexible yields. The only way to increase production was to place more land under cultivation. This meant borrowing, typically at rates of more than 7 percent. When the government foolishly imposed price controls on grain in 1539, the whole enterprise became uneconomical and Castile embarked on the course that would, in the next generation, make it a net importer of grains from abroad.

Manufacturing, too, suffered from inflation and government intervention. Castile's textile, ceramics, and metals industries found ready customers abroad, but as the reign progressed, prices rose to uneconomic levels. For reasons that remain unclear in this age of demographic growth, labor shortages held down production and quality declined as prices rose. The Cortes tried to lower prices by banning textile exports and permitting imports. It reversed the ban in 1558 after the industry collapsed, but the Castilian trade in both wool and finished cloths never fully recovered. In time Castile would become a net importer of manufactured goods as well as of grain. Though the general level of prosperity remained high when Charles died, the seeds of future problems had been planted.

In the kingdom of Aragon the trade of Barcelona had begun to decline in the fifteenth century. Charles made matters worse by consistently denying Catalan merchants the right to trade in the New World and by allowing the Genoese to dominate the trade of Naples and Sicily, in part as a reward for the defection of Andrea Doria in 1528. Driven out of their natural markets in Italy, the Catalans turned to the wool trade in Castile, where they faced an elaborate series of import duties and other barriers that were not applied to their northern European competitors. But if the transient prosperity of Castile eluded them, its inflation did not. Catalan manufacturers found it increasingly difficult to match the prices of their foreign competitors, and gradually declined as well. If the economic legacy of the reign in Castile held the potential for disasters to come, in Catalonia it meant near collapse while the Emperor yet lived.

The intellectual and cultural legacy of Charles's reign in the Spanish kingdoms is more difficult to assess. The shadow of the Inquisition clouds our perception, and its influence raises questions that may in the end be unanswerable. In the beginning, the arrival of the young King and his Burgundian entourage brought new tastes and interests to the Spanish world. Exposure to the art and artists of the Netherlands leavened a conservative and rather narrow artistic tradition, as did subsequent borrowings from the Italian Renaissance. Charles himself patronized Italian artists and built a palace in the incongruous form of a classical temple on the grounds of the Moorish Alhambra. By the end of the reign, a rich tradition of Spanish painting had begun to emerge, but for all its sharp-eyed observation of daily life, Spanish art remained overwhelmingly religious in theme and conservative in its iconography. This reflected the taste of Spanish patrons, many of whom were ecclesiastics, and had little or nothing to do with the Inquisition.

At the same time, many of Charles's early advisors were not only humanists, but admirers of the Dutch scholar Erasmus. The Erasmian approach to humanism, and with it the great man's criticisms of clerical abuse, flowed into Spain and gained currency among some elements of the intellectual elite. A few of these people, including the prominent scholars Diego de Uceda and Juan de Valdés, were tried or investigated by the Inquisition, and by the mid-1530s Spanish Erasmianism had all but disappeared. Later, at the very end of the reign, the Holy Office began to investigate what appeared to be Protestants in Sevilla and Valladolid. Charles, by then in his decline, enthusiastically approved.[5] After a series of persecutions in the early years of Philip II, this movement, if movement it was, disappeared as well. The success of the inquisitors in these cases convinced scholars of the eighteenth and nineteenth centuries that the Inquisition forced Spanish intellectual development into narrow and unproductive paths that cut Spain off from the rest of Europe and helped account for its supposed backwardness in their own day. The truth is somewhat more complex.

Charles V vigorously supported the Inquisition. When he came to the throne, the institution's many Spanish opponents asked him to modify such practices as concealing accusations from the accused, denying them access to the sacraments or legal counsel while under investigation, and paying inquisitors from the proceeds of confiscations. Adrian of Utrecht, his new Inquisitor General, refused all proposed reforms with the King's blessing. It is also true that, having solved the 'problem' of the *conversos* to its own satisfaction, the tribunal turned its attention to heresy in the

1520s. Its efforts, however, were limited by a shortage of potential victims. Few Spaniards seemed interested in heterodox thought, much less in Protestantism.

The persecutions of the 1520s and 1530s were directed primarily against a movement known as Illuminism that concentrated on mental prayer and a kind of mystic contemplation that aroused concern among the more conservative clerics. Originating in Franciscan spirituality, it had nothing to do with Luther, but some of its advocates attempted to use Erasmianism for their own purposes. This brought the inquisitors to people like Valdés, who, in his *Dialogue of Christian Doctrine* (1530) did in fact echo some of Luther's earlier ideas. That Luther and Erasmus had long been at odds on such fundamental issues as justification seems to have eluded the inquisitors. It is clear from these episodes, and from the later trials in Sevilla and Valladolid, that the fathers of the Inquisition understood little of Protestant teachings. Only a handful of those convicted during the 1560s can be described as Protestants; the rest held objectionable ideas of other kinds. The Inquisition, then, may have destroyed Spanish Protestanism, but the movement was in any case small and probably incapable of dramatic expansion. Equally coercive methods in the Netherlands were temporarily successful under Charles V. Under Philip II they achieved little or nothing against a Protestantism that had found rich sustenance in the local culture.

Spanish humanism, on the other hand, survived the attack on Erasmus. Its roots predated him and most of its exponents, both before and after the persecutions of the 1530s, owed their intellectual formation to Italy, notably the University of Bologna. The Erasmian suspicion of formal reason and of Aristotle in particular – a suspicion largely responsible for the Inquisition's hostility – never appealed to a majority of Spanish scholars. In any case Erasmus, like most writers, fell out of fashion after his death and remained relatively unappreciated until the authors of the Enlightenment revived him for their own purposes in the eighteenth century. It is therefore unlikely that the persecution of Erasmians significantly altered the course of Spanish scholarship. The effect of the Inquisition on literature seems to have been minimal as well. Under Philip II it investigated devotional writers including St Teresa and Luis de Granada, but the century after Charles's death is still regarded as the golden age of Spanish literature.

The Inquisition threatened already unpopular lines of inquiry and handed a nasty weapon to those who practiced academic politics as a blood sport, but as an institution of repression it was unique only in its consistency and in its adherence to what passed for legal norms. Other sixteenth-century states, both Catholic and Protestant, tried to control religious ideas with equal ruthlessness and effect. If the reign of Charles V influenced Spanish learning in any measureable way, it was in the flowering of political thought inspired by the transformation of frontier Spain into a world empire. Such thinkers as Francisco de Vitoria, Alfonso de Valdés, Juan Luis Vives, and Juan Ginés de Sepúlveda struggled heroically with fundamental issues of governance and political morality and produced a body of work which, though it rejected machiavellianism and remained well within the Aristotelian and Christian traditions, profoundly effected political theorists in the rest of Europe.

THE NEW WORLD

In the Americas the reign of Charles V brought cataclysmic transformations unequalled in historical times. Under Ferdinand and Isabella, Castilians had continued the process of exploration begun by Columbus, but effective occupation was limited to the islands of the Caribbean. The beginning of Charles's reign (1519–21) saw the conquest of Mexico by a small force under Hernán Cortés. A decade later (1531–32), Francisco Pizarro and his men conquered the empire of the Incas in the Andean highlands. Lesser expeditions claimed the spaces between, and by 1558 much of south and central America was firmly under Spanish control. Everywhere, the suppression of native cultures was brutal and, to a remarkable degree, complete. The Spanish thought it their duty to spread the Christian faith and believed that this could not be done unless they separated native Americans from their traditional ways. They threw down idols, destroyed temples, and worked tirelessly to erase the memory of ancient beliefs. Indigeneous languages perished or went underground. Spanish became the *lingua franca* of the Americas, and cities were rebuilt according to the quasi-Roman model that had evolved during the reconquest of Castile from the Moors.

In Mexico, and to a lesser degree in other parts of the Americas, demographic catastrophe added to the disruption. Owing largely to the introduction of such European diseases as smallpox, central Mexico lost at least 60 percent of its population between 1530 and 1568.[6] The arrival of new diseases was only part of a larger biological exchange that would eventually change the ecology and eating habits of the Old World as well as the New. Spanish livestock added meat to the diet of Americans while altering forever the landscape in which they lived. Maize, potatoes, cassava, and a host of other vegetable foods found their way to Europe and Africa with great, though delayed, effects on demography and nutrition. None of this requires further comment here, nor is it essential to describe the growth of a world market and the globalization of European conflicts that followed. Few would doubt that the Spanish conquest of the New World was among the most important events in the history of the world.

The Emperor, of course, contributed little or nothing to the conquest and, like most of his contemporaries, did not foresee its results. He was simply King of Castile at a time when entrepreneurial adventurers added whole continents to his realm. Those continents, however, could be made to produce badly needed revenue. They had also to be governed, and Charles was determined to institutionalize the conquests in ways that would ensure royal control and provide good government as he understood it. Typically, he preferred existing models to Utopian innovation.

Ferdinand and Isabella had decreed that the Indians should retain their lands, and that all lands not actually occupied by them should become possessions of the Crown. Some of these Crown lands were granted to individual *conquistadores* who, according to Castilian custom, organized the properties into towns protected by royal charters. Though every effort was made to prevent the emergence of great lordships on the Andalusian model, local authority continued to be exercised on a temporary basis by individual *conquistadores* or by the councils of the towns they had founded. Abuses were legion. Indian land was confiscated, and the Indians themselves enslaved, though Isabella had forbidden most Indian slavery in 1500. Colonial goods often reached Spain without paying the tax to which the Crown was entitled. In 1503 the monarchs centralized all trade and communication with the New World through the *Casa de Contratación* in Sevilla, but the administration of American affairs and judicial appeals from the colonies remained under the personal control of the Bishop of Burgos, Juan Rodríguez de Fonseca. Erring *conquistadores* might occasionally be punished, but the system as a whole was makeshift and unsatisfactory.

When Fonseca died in 1524, Charles used the occasion to establish a system of government based firmly on traditional models that would endure until the revolutions of the nineteenth century. He began by creating a Council of the Indies with administrative, judicial, and ecclesiastical authority over all matters originating in the New World. New Spain

(Mexico) and Peru were eventually organized as kingdoms ruled separately by the King of Castile, but governed by viceroys who served as the
King's personal representatives. The system was modelled on that of the
medieval Aragonese empire, but the authority of American viceroys was
more limited than those of Aragon, Catalonia, Valencia, and the Italian
kingdoms. In America the King's judicial authority and some of his
administrative powers were granted to *audiencias* established on the
Castilian model, perhaps because Charles feared that isolation might
encourage viceregal independence if constitutional checks were not in
place. In practice, viceroys and their *audiencias* often collaborated, and
the system as a whole worked well.

Its chief defect was imposed by distance. A message or petition might
require months or even years to reach Spain from Peru. Conciliar deliberations were rarely speedy, and under Charles V, the Council's recom-
mendations might take weeks to reach the King if he were campaigning
abroad. The return trip was no faster. Under Philip II an elaborate system of annual convoys to and from the New World was established, but
its primary purpose was to protect the bullion shipments that became
regular only after the Emperor's death. Under Charles, the profits from
his new realms came largely in the form of unpredictable windfalls from
the conquests of Mexico and Peru.

Organizing the empire proved easier than establishing justice and
good government within it. Castile was the first western nation since
Roman times to impose its rule on vast populations whose cultures were
wholly unlike its own. The treatment of these indigeneous peoples created moral and practical dilemmas of great complexity. From the beginning, the Crown had hoped to prevent the uncontrolled exploitation of
its new subjects by the *conquistadores*, in part for moral and religious reasons and in part because only the *conquistadores* wanted to see the development of a New World aristocracy on the Castilian model, based on
Indian labor and largely independent of royal control. Unfortunately,
Isabella's ban on Indian slavery had been virtually meaningless. Indians
who 'rebelled' against the Spanish or committed other crimes were
exempt from her decree, and the conquerors found it easy to create
pretexts for creating new slaves. If this failed, they fell back on the
encomienda, an institution that dated from the *reconquista* of medieval
Spain. New subjects were given *en encomienda* to their conquerors who
were to protect them and provide for their conversion in return for dues
or labor services. In American practice this all too often meant forced
labor in the mines and elsewhere. By the time Charles V came to the

throne, the *encomienda* system, together with slavery, had already led to untold deaths in the Caribbean.

Since 1511 members of the Dominican order, and in particular the great Bartolomé de Las Casas, had campaigned vigorously on behalf of the oppressed Indians. His efforts culminated in a famous debate at the University of Salamanca in 1550 in which he argued that the Indians met Aristotle's standard of rational beings and therefore could not legally be enslaved. Charles V agreed; his government had in fact been working for years to destroy both Indian slavery and the *encomienda* system. In 1542 the so-called New Laws forbade any further enslavement of Indians and forced the owners of existing slaves to show proof of ownership. Most *encomiendas* were abolished outright, and it was decreed that those remaining would expire on the death of their present holders. The colonists responded with a flood of protests, and in Peru, with a bloody revolt led by Gonzalo Pizarro that took more than three years to suppress. Faced with chaos, the government made concessions on the *encomienda* issue, but held firm on the prohibition of Indian slavery. In 1549 another decree prohibited *encomenderos* from substituting forced labor in the mines for tribute. Eventually, a system known as the *repartimiento* developed by which Indians were paid wages for work conducted under government supervision. It, too, was susceptible to great abuse, but by 1560 both Indian slavery and the *encomienda* system had largely passed from the scene.

This body of legislation shows Charles's government at its best and compares favorably with the efforts of other colonial powers, but it was neither perfect nor overly effective. The native population of the Spanish empire, like the peasants of old Europe, continued to be oppressed in a variety of ingenious ways and no effort was made to discourage the enslavement of Africans. The reign of Charles V did not create an ideal society in the New World or anywhere else, but its achievements were substantial. With a steadinesss of purpose appropriate to the difficulty of their task, the Emperor and his advisors consolidated the conquests, asserted his authority over an area many times greater than all of Europe, and provided it with a government that was, by contemporary standards at least, just, honest, and efficient.

ITALY

Sicily, Naples, and Sardinia, the Italian kingdoms that formed part of the Emperor's Aragonese inheritance, were each governed throughout most of his reign by Spanish viceroys assisted by Spanish administrators. Titled landowners (*baroni*) exercised local control in town and country with the assistance of bandit gangs whose organization and behavior have been said to resemble the modern mafia. Aragonese policy had been to favor the *baroni* while neutralizing their ability to interfere with the larger concerns of the monarchy. Charles and his viceroys followed the same course. Moreover, the cultural shock that would eventually complicate relations between the Spanish and the Dutch did not develop, in part because the Spanish generally treated the Italians as equals.[7] Perhaps for these reasons, all three of the kingdoms accepted his rule without significant protest. Disorders at the very beginning of the reign were put down without difficulty. Later, in Naples, a faction of nobles supported the French during the invasion of 1527, suffering confiscations and in some cases death as a result of their attachment to the Angevin cause. Their lands were given to the Emperor's military leaders, Doria, de Leyva, Gonzaga, and Colonna, whose families quickly became indistinguishable from the *baroni*, at least in local politics. Popular riots, usually over local issues, remained fairly common in both Naples and Sicily, and there was a brief revolt against the Viceroy of Naples in 1547, but no serious threat to Spanish sovereignty emerged until the 1640s.

The problems faced by the viceroys in Italy were of another kind. One of the worst, from their perspective, was the maintenance of public order. Charles's governors in all three kingdoms strove mightily to control banditry, but not even the energetic Don Pedro de Toledo at Naples succeeded. In 20 years, he claimed to have killed 18 000 bandits, but they were as numerous as ever when he died in 1553. The chief result of his effort was the revolt of 1547. Protected both by the *baroni*, who used them as enforcers, and by poor people who saw them as heroes or potential allies capable of mediating their disputes, the bandits had become too essential to the system to be destroyed or even controlled.

The Spanish Inquisition created other issues. Ferdinand of Aragon had introduced it in Sicily in 1487 and in Sardinia five years later. He brought the inquisitors to Naples in 1509, but was forced to withdraw them in the face of implacable Neapolitan resistance. In 1542, the year in which Paul III revived the Papal Inquisition to combat the growth of Italian Protestantism, Charles V tried to reintroduce the Spanish version at Naples. He sympathized with papal intiatives, but preferred the Spanish Inquisition because his government and not the Pope controlled it. Once again, the Neapolitans rioted and the Inquisition was once more withdrawn, never to be revived.

In Sicily, by way of contrast, the Inquisition enjoyed a certain popularity. False denunciations offered yet another means of pursuing vendetta against one's neighbors and were said to be ten times more common than in Spain, but the Sicilians never accepted the practice of hanging San Benitos in the churches as a symbol of a family's shame, and resolutely opposed capital punishment for religious crimes. After Tunis, Charles removed the Inquisition's jurisdiction over capital crimes for five years in return for 250 000 ducats from the Sicilian parliament, but reneged on the agreement when a Protestant was found at Messina in 1541. From 1542 to 1580, the Sicilian tribunal executed 30 Protestants, most of them in the reign of Philip II.[8] Sicily did not at this time enjoy a conspicuous reputation for learning, and the impact of its Inquisition on non-religious thought appears to have been negligible. Naples, on the other hand, boasted an active humanist circle until the 1540s when it began to decline without inquisitorial pressure.

To economic historians, the most important issue in Charles's governance of the Italian kingdoms has been the degree to which his fiscal policies contributed to the decline of the Italian south. Sardinia, of course, was poor and remained so, contributing little to the revenues of the Crown. Naples and Sicily experienced population growth and relative prosperity through most of the sixteenth century, but declined precipitately in the seventeenth. There can be no doubt that taxes increased greatly in both kingdoms during the reign of Charles V. The number and size of extraordinary aids or *donativi* grew, especially in Naples, and a host of new excises were imposed beginning in the 1550s. Still, if it is true that the tax burden on Sicily during this period was not especially harsh and that even Naples was taxed below its capacity, lack of investment in agriculture and commerce may have been a more important reason for the growing backwardness of the south than taxes. As in Castile, government securities seem to have absorbed the bulk of investment capital. Charles had granted the best trading opportunities to foreigners from Genoa and Milan, while the availability of cheap labor made agricultural investment superfluous. Real economic decline came only in the seventeenth century when exports and agricultural yields dropped for reasons that had little to do with state policy, while taxes continued to increase and the government began the suicidal practice of taxing or withholding payment on its own securities.[9] In Naples, the most immediate consequence of the government's fiscal policy was the enormous growth of the city at the expense of the countryside. Both the ordinary and extraordinary revenues voted by parliament came from the hearth tax or *focatico* which was not levied on city dwellers. The response to this exemption was as overwhelming as it was predictable, and Viceroy Toledo had to launch an expensive program of public works as the city expanded.

The most important consequence of the Emperor's reign in southern Italy is that it tied the region firmly to Spain and promoted a degree of loyalty that lasted into the nineteenth century. That relationship was formalized in 1555 by the creation of a Council of Italy based on the model of the Council of the Indies. It was a mixed legacy. Charles's viceroys and those who followed understood the cultures of all three kingdoms and served successfully as referees among their various factions. They provided a greater measure of defense against the pirates of North Africa than any of the three kingdoms could afford on its own, and their public works contributed to the amenities of Naples and Palermo. Perhaps the famous lament of Benedetto Croce for his native land can stand as their epitaph: 'Our only regret is that, since the kingdom of Naples had to join itself to some more powerful state, it should have fallen into the hands of the one least able to invigorate its economic life and with which it could only share its poverty and lack of industrial and commercial capacity.'[10]

Charles V held the kingdoms of southern Italy by hereditary right. Northern Italy remained a patchwork of republics and principalities in which he claimed only Milan, not in his own name, but as a fief of the Holy Roman Empire. By 1530, the success of his wars with Francis I allowed Charles to restore Francesco Maria Sforza as his vassal at Milan. The imperial armies had also achieved a real, though not unchallengeable, military superiority in Italy as a whole. It remained for the Emperor to consolidate his position by drawing the rulers of other Italian states into his orbit of patronage, making them allies and dependants and neutralizing any powers that could not be bought.

The landlocked Duchy of Milan dominated the Lombard plain and stretched northward to the Alpine passes into Switzerland. Its strategic usefulness to the Empire of Charles V depended largely on friendship with Genoa, whose port connected it with the western Mediterranean. After bribing Andrea Doria to abandon the siege of Naples in 1528, Charles took steps to ensure that never again would the city's naval and financial power be harnessed by his enemies. Lucrative contracts tied the Genoese fleet to the imperial service. Generous grants of land in the kingdom of Naples went to the leading families, while *asientos* and trade privileges drew the city's merchants into the tangled web of imperial finance. By 1575 Genoese aristocrats found that 40 percent of their total wealth was invested in loans to Spain while 80 percent of the city's long-distance trade involved Spanish territories.[11]

To the east, Charles maintained good relations with Venice after 1529, and earned the gratitude of the Este at Ferrara by reconciling their bitter quarrel with the papacy. He raised the title of Ferrante Gonzaga at Mantua to duke, confirmed his succession to Montferrat, and gave him prominent commands in the imperial army including, for a time, the post of lieutenant general in Milan. On the west, he favored the interests of Emanuele Filiberto of Savoy, whose ancestral lands were occupied by the French. Raised largely at Charles's court, Savoy was given command of the army in the Netherlands in 1553 and appointed to the council of state. When Charles abdicated, Emmanuele Filiberto succeeded Mary of Hungary as Regent of the Netherlands and recovered his duchy at Cateau-Cambrésis after winning the battle of St Quentin for Philip II. All three of these princely dynasties remained Habsburg clients under Spanish rule.

The papacy was a more difficult problem, in part because it was controlled by different Italian families in succession, and in part because of the unavoidable tension between the Emperor's policies and those of the popes. Throughout the Middle Ages popes had opposed the expansion of imperial authority in Italy because it threatened the Papal States. The Sack of Rome showed what could happen even when the Emperor intended no harm. After 1529, with Charles firmly in control of southern Italy and rapidly extending his authority over the north, his power appeared more ominous than ever. Beleaguered popes were all too easily tempted by a French alliance even if it meant the scandal of an unacknowledged bond with France's allies, the Turks and Protestants. We have also seen that frequent changes of policy by the Emperor and several popes on the issue of a Council caused further stress in papal–imperial relations.

For obvious reasons, the Emperor preferred to resolve these problems without resorting to military force. Through the judicious use of favors he could draw the Pope's vassals into his own web of patronage and use their loyalty to put pressure on a recalcitrant Pope. This tactic was especially tempting in the case of families like the Colonna, who held lands in Naples as well as in the Papal States, though it failed conspicuously in 1527 and again in 1541. It was better to extend patronage to the popes themselves. Sixteenth-century popes typically belonged to one or another of the powerful Italian families and used their office to strengthen the political position of their relatives. By granting or withholding support for their schemes, Charles could influence policy for the duration of their pontificate. Different arrangements, of course, had to be made with each new incumbent. Charles was nevertheless able to construct firm alliances with at least two important Italian clans whose influence survived their papal relatives. In 1530, as part of a broader *rapprochement* after the Ladies' Peace, Charles helped Clement VII to restore the Medici at Florence and named Alessandro de'Medici hereditary duke. Alessandro was promised the hand of Charles's illegitimate daughter Margaret, then only eight. Clement in return foreswore all alliances with the French, granted Charles the proceeds of the *cruzada*, or crusade tax in Castile, and crowned him Emperor. The imperial army had to reduce the city by siege. When Alessandro was murdered in 1537, Charles confirmed his young cousin Cosimo I as Duke and encouraged him to marry Leonor, daughter of Pedro de Toledo, the Viceroy of Naples. Later, in 1554 Cosimo commanded an imperial army that destroyed the Republic of Siena. In negotiations complicated by disagreement between Charles and his son Philip, Philip became Vicar of Siena and promptly granted it in fief to Cosimo, who ruled it thereafter. Tuscany remained firmly allied with the Habsburgs until the defection of Grand Duke Ferdinand after 1589.

Relations with the Farnese at Parma and Piacenza were more difficult. Pope Paul III detached these territories on the southern borders of Milan from the Papal States and granted them to his son Pier Luigi Farnese in 1545. The latter's flirtations with France earned the distrust of Charles V. Pier Luigi was assasinated in 1547, possibly with the Emperor's connivance, and when his son Ottavio succeeded him, Charles seized Piacenza. In this case, the Emperor's concern for the security of neighboring Milan had caused him to overreact. Ottavio, who had married the Emperor's illegitimate daughter Margaret after she had been spared a wedding with Alessandro de'Medici, had no desire to quarrel with his Habsburg in-laws. He tied himself to the rising star of Philip II, who returned Piacenza to him in 1556. Both his wife and his son Alessandro Farnese, Prince of Parma, would serve the King with distinction in the Netherlands.

These arrangements, carefully tended under Philip II, complemented the achievement of direct rule in Milan. When Francesco Maria Sforza died without heirs in 1535, Charles insisted that the duchy revert to the Empire. He appointed the Marquis del Vasto lieutenant general, and in 1540 formally transferred the city and its territories to Prince Philip. The 'New Constitutions' of 1541 reformed the duchy's legal system, and when the confusion created by the Peace of Crépy ended with the death of the Duke of Orléans in 1545, Charles promulgated the Ordinances of Worms which reformed the city's governance and tied it more closely to the imperial administration. Milan, however, remained something of an anomaly. For years to come its exposed position and strategic importance caused it to be governed by the chief military commander in northern Italy. Though taxed to the very limits of its considerable wealth, all of its revenues were consumed locally, leaving no surplus for the imperial treasury as a whole. As in the rest of Italy, economic life stagnated, especially during the seventeenth century, but Milan remained loyal to the Habsburgs, perhaps because day-to-day administration was left to a tight-knit oligarchy whose symbiotic relationship with the monarchy recalls that of the Neapolitan barons. Milan, together with the system of patronage developed by Charles V among the princes of northern Italy and direct Habsburg rule in the south, formed the basis of the Spanish hegemony that lasted until the Austrian invasion of 1706.

To many Italians, including Machiavelli and Francesco Guicciardini, the reign of Charles V marked the end of Italian freedom. To intellectual historians from the Enlightenment to the present, it also marked the end of the Renaissance. This view, which in its simplest form held that the Renaissance was destroyed by the Counter-Reformation, has become difficult to sustain, but few would deny that the vitality of humanism as a movement had greatly diminished by mid-century.

The revival of the Papal Inquisition in 1542 together with the publication of the *Index Librorum Prohibitorum* (Index of Prohibited Books) marked the rejection of Contarini's policy of compromise and the beginning of a new and repressive phase of Catholic reform. The leading spirit of this movement was Cardinal Gianpietro Caraffa, who became Pope Paul IV in 1555. The Papal Inquisition labored primarily in the states of northern Italy not directly ruled by Charles V, though it was firmly resisted in Venice and its territories. It limited the growth of Italian Protestantism, but its effect on learning as a whole, like that of the Spanish Inquisition, has been questioned by modern scholarship. As in Spain, the Inquisition remained a trap for the unwary and a weapon in the arsenal of academic and eclesiastical politicians, but it did not destroy scholarship. Its worst effect may have been to encourage self-censorship by speculative thinkers whose work had theological implications. The efficiency of the *Index*, too, has been exaggerated. It forced Italian authors to publish their heterodox works abroad, but did not stop prohibited books from appearing with regularity in Italian libraries. The chilling effect of these measures should not be minimized, but they do not explain everything. If the Italian Renaissance faded during the reign of Charles V, it was at least in part because the movement's initial impetus had vanished. There were no new classics to be discovered, and civic humanism, so important in the early years of the movement, seemed meaningless after the Italian cities had lost their freedom.

THE NETHERLANDS

Charles V spent relatively little time in his native land, a total of only 55 months in a reign of nearly 40 years. While occupied elsewhere, he governed the 17 provinces through two regents: his aunt, Margaret of Austria (1517–30) and his sister, Mary of Hungary, who ruled from 1530 to 1555. Margaret was a natural politician whose charm and affability recalled her father, Maximilian I. Mary, the widow of Louis of Hungary, combined energy, courage, and intelligence with a hard, unforgiving temperament. Though both were capable and loyal, neither succeeded in making their government popular. The Emperor's endless demands for money, his tendency to subordinate the interests of the Netherlands to the broader concerns of empire, the destructive incursions of France and Gelre, and his religious policies tried his subject's patience to the limits. When Charles was physically present, they bowed to his will; in his absence they sometimes treated his female relatives with less respect.

The achievements and failures of the reign must therefore be seen against a background of almost constant tension between the central government and its subjects. The temptation to see that tension, or the government of Charles V itself, as a cause of the great revolt that devastated the Netherlands in the reign of Philip II, should, however, be avoided. Charles and his regents were at all times careful to consult with members of the dominant elites and protect their interests. Constitutional norms were respected. The reign created at least some of the pre-conditions of that revolt, but when Charles abdicated neither the revolt nor the rise of the Dutch Republic was in any sense pre-ordained.

Among the government's achievements, the most obvious was the physical expansion of Habsburg territories in the Netherlands, a legacy of the wars with France and Gelre. We have seen that the war of 1521–22 enabled Charles to annex Tournai with its bishopric, and Friesland, which until then had never acknowledged an overlord. Like the other provinces of the north and east, Friesland had hoped to preserve its independence by allying with Gelre, but Gelre could not protect a region so distant and so isolated from its own heartland. In time it became obvious that Duke Charles of Gelre could not protect even those allies whose lands were close to his own. In 1527 an invasion by Gelre inspired the Bishop of Utrecht to place his diocese, the province of Utrecht, and Overijssel under Habsburg rule. The year ended with a Habsburg counter-invasion of Gelderland and the treaty of Gorinchem (1528), by which the childless Duke agreed to leave Gelre to the Emperor when he died. This solved nothing, for Gelre once again allied itself with France in the war of 1536. The campaign of that year added Groningen, the Ommelanden, and Drenthe to the Habsburg realms. Then, when Duke Charles died at last in 1538 after a reign of 46 years, the States of Gelre refused to accept his will, repudiated the treaty of Gorinchem, and elected William 'the Rich,' Duke of Cleves-Jülich as their ruler. The new arrangement did not survive the bitter campaigns of 1542–43. The Regent's armies drove Martin van Rossem from Flanders and Holland, and when Charles personally invaded Cleves in 1543, Duke William thought himself lucky to cede Gelderland to the Habsburgs in return for the preservation of his hereditary lands. With the annexation of Cambrai in the same year, the map of the Low Countries assumed the form it would retain until the establishment of the Dutch Republic. Only the great bishopric of Liège and the little county of Ravenstein remained independent.

The expansion of Habsburg territories in the Netherlands, though impressive, involved no grand design and little forethought. It was largely the result of opportunism and of the Emperor's larger success in the wars with France. Still less does there appear to have been any attempt at transforming the provinces of the Netherlands into anything resembling a modern state. If anything, Charles's policies in his native land may inadvertently have strengthened the provinces at the expense of the central government and taught them how to act in concert with the nobility when their interests were threatened.

Institutionally, the Emperor made a number of adjustments, most of them when he came to the Netherlands in 1531–32 after the death of Margaret of Austria. He defined and increased the authority of the bailiffs who represented his government in the towns, and limited that of the *stadholders*, who were encouraged to reside at Brussels under the watchful eye of the new Regent, Mary. He also began the process of separating the Privy Council and the Council of State. The Privy Council had long been the preserve of lawyers with its own headquarters, its own bureaucracy, and a well-established appellate jurisdiction; by 1548 it had acquired a separate presidency as well. The Council of State remained as it had been under Margaret: a committee of high nobles who advised the Regent on foreign policy. In June of that year, Charles also persuaded the Diet of Augsburg to declare the provinces of the Netherlands a separate unit exempt from imperial legislation and jurisdiction. They would continue to provide troops and taxes, but would be otherwise indpendent. This move was clearly related to the succession issue, then being hotly debated within the Habsburg family. If the Netherlands went to Charles's son Philip II and the Empire to Ferdinand of Austria, institutional separation was needed. Shortly thereafter, all of the provinces were given representative bodies, a privilege hitherto reserved for the hereditary lands.

Charles was also committed to legal reform. Beginning in October, 1531, he promulgated new laws dealing with commerce, heresy, the exploitation of wilderness areas, and other matters. None of his legislation, though badly needed, could supercede ancient 'customs' without the consent of the provincial estates. Unfortunately, a precise understanding of those customs remained elusive. Like other parts of Europe, the Netherlands possessed a body of customary law that varied from province to province. Much of it had never been written down, much less codified. The resulting disputes prolonged legal proceedings and made it difficult to integrate new laws with the old. Other states faced the same problem in the sixteenth century, but under Charles V, the Netherlands experienced something of a legal renaissance. In 1531 and again in 1540 he ordered the examination and codification of all existing laws. A massive effort by jurists trained at the universities in Roman law laid the groundwork for this enormous project, but provincial resistance ensured that it would be many decades before their work could become the basis of a true legal code.

These changes were important, but the engine driving Charles's policy in the Netherlands was never institutional reform. His consuming need for money controlled his actions and ultimately forced him into a new relationship with the provinces. Revenues from the Netherlands increased dramatically throughout the reign, primarily as a result of the many 'extraordinary' *aides* or *beden* needed to fund the wars. Debt increased even more rapidly. The provinces, when called upon to produce more money, resorted to issuing bonds or *renten* against expected revenues. Flanders began issuing bonds against both existing *beden* and those that had not yet been technically voted in 1544. Holland followed suit in 1553. The bonds, based solidly on funded debt, paid between 6 percent and 7 percent and became a popular investment for the office-holding class in the towns. The central government, whose own credit was bad and growing worse, found it convenient to shift debt to the provinces whose credit remained good. One consequence of this shift was that bankers began to establish direct financial relationships with provinces rather than with the Regent at Brussels. Another was that, in time, provincial officials acquired more control over both the collection and disbursement of funds. Traditionally, the collection of 'ordinary' revenues had been the responsibility of a Receiver employed by the central government. By 1552, however, 'extraordinary' revenues had become 12 times greater than the 'ordinary,' and these, by necessity, were collected by officers of the provincial states. At the same time, the Emperor's desperate need for funds forced him to provide guarantees that money collected would be spent only on the purposes for which it had been voted. By the end of the reign, both the credit and the authority of the provincial states had strengthened enormously.[12]

The provincial states also found that, if the government's needs were great enough, they could sometimes force the Regent to support their interests against those of the dynasty. This did not happen often. It required cooperation from the nobles, but if a province or group of provinces spoke with a single voice, the government sometimes listened. In 1536, for example, Holland was able to thwart Charles's attempts to interfere in the succession of Christian III of Denmark. The Emperor's involvement with Denmark had a long history. Charles's sister Isabella had married Christian II, whose anti-aristocratic policies led to his over-throw in 1523. Christian's uncle led the revolt and ruled for ten years as Frederick I. When Frederick died, Charles hoped to secure the Danish succession for his own niece, the daughter of Christian II and Isabella, but the Danes preferred Frederick's son, Christian III. To protect him-self against Habsburg ambitions, Christian formed alliances with Gelre and with the city of Lübeck, Holland's chief rival for the Baltic trade. The Hollanders concluded that Christian would win in spite of Charles, and that he would retaliate against the Habsburgs by blocking Dutch ships from entering the Baltic. Fearing the loss of their most vital trade, the States and nobility of Holland, supported by several other provinces, successfully obstructed a proposed campaign against Denmark. The affair so embarassed Mary of Hungary that she asked to be relieved of her office, but Charles wisely refused to accept her resignation.[13]

The growing ability to control their own finances, and even on rare occasions to influence imperial policy, indicates that at least some of the provinces were individually more unified and cohesive in political terms than they had been at the beginning of the reign. They were certainly more creditworthy. Against this must be set the ongoing internal struggles over trade privileges, canal navigation, protection of the herring fishery, and a host of other issues that would inhibit cooperation among them for decades to come. William of Orange would discover that, even in the midst of the mortal struggle with Spain, the problem of governance under the Republic was little different than it had been in the time of the Emperor.[14]

But if the Emperor did little to modernize and strengthen the institutions of the Low Countries as a whole, his government created a number of grievances that were unresolved at the time of his death and would be augmented by Philip II. The suspicion and hostility aroused by the government's fiscal demands need little comment. Most of the money raised was spent on the defense of the Netherlands, but tax rates were high and most Netherlanders preferred to believe that their money was being used for purposes unrelated to their needs. Some, including Erasmus, thought that the government provoked wars solely for the purpose of raising taxes.[15] Similar notions had been current at least since the time of Charles the Bold and were shared by the subjects of other rulers, but neither Charles nor his regents did anything to allay them. Conspiratorial theories aside, the reality of taxation was bad enough. Taxes in some regions had increased fourfold during the reign; in others as much as twelvefold.[16] Real wealth and population began to decline after 1540 throughout the Netherlands and unrest became common.

Much of the trouble was minor and easily controlled by the local authorities; the revolt at Ghent was more serious. A radical faction known as the *Creesers* (Screamers) seized power in 1540 amid scenes of mob violence and summary executions. They refused to pay an extraordinary *bede* that had been accepted by the rest of Flanders and let it be known that they would not accept 'the rule of a woman,' specifically Mary of Hungary. When he arrived in the Netherlands after touring France, Charles invaded his native city in person, levelled one of its neighborhoods, and summarily deprived it of its ancient privileges. This object lesson in imperial ruthlessness had the desired effect. There was major rioting at Antwerp in 1554, but no more rebellions sponsored by city governments.

Far more serious was the religious issue. The Netherlands had a long tradition of lay piety that emphasized mental prayer and other forms of contact with God that did not involve ceremonies or the sacraments. The *beguines*, the Brothers and Sisters of the Common Life, and even Erasmian humanism promoted such tendencies while stressing Scripture reading and the imitation of Christ through good works, many of which were performed under the sponsorship of civic corporations. The anticlericalism implied by these attitudes ran deep. Preachers and humanists excoriated the vices of the clergy and attacked their privileges. Laymen especially resented the clerical exemption from excise taxes, which enabled monastic houses to compete unfairly in a variety of trades. In this environment, heterodox ideas, some borrowed from Luther and others grown locally, found ready acceptance even before the confrontation at Worms.

Charles, as hereditary ruler of the Netherlands, had no intention of allowing such notions to take permanent root. Beginning in 1521 he issued a series of *placards* demanding ferocious penalties for heresy and prohibiting heretical or merely offensive books. The *placards* offended his subjects because they appeared to bolster ecclesiastical privilege and infringe the authority of their local governments. The legal principle behind them was that heresy was not an ordinary crime, but *crimen lesae majestatis divinae* or treason against God. As in cases of treason against the prince, normal judicial procedures did not apply. Guilt would be established by a panel of clerical inquisitors under the guidance of two laymen, the President of the Grand Council of Mechelen and a member of the Council of Brabant. The guilty would then be 'relaxed' to the secular authorities for punishment.

From the beginning, secular authorities reacted to these measures by setting minor penalties for what, in the government's eyes, were major crimes. In some cases, heretics were released with a good-natured warning to keep their mouths shut. Local privilege and anticlericalism aside, it soon became obvious that many magistrates – and ordinary people as well – disapproved of torture and execution in matters of belief as a matter of principle. The magistrates were not heretics. Like most Netherlanders, they remained Catholic, but repressive policies that had been accepted in Spain found little support in the very different culture of the Low Countries. In 1529, an exasperated government reacted to magisterial obstruction with another *placard* that removed all discretion from local courts in the setting of penalties and prescribed death as the sole punishment for heresy.

In 1530 Charles used his new friendship with Pope Clement VII to acquire the right to nominate bishops within his territories. He had long felt that effective bishops were the key to suppressing heresy, and had already requested the establishment of new dioceses at Brussels, Leiden, Middelburg, Ghent, and Bruges. That request, however, had been ignored. In the 1540s Charles asked the faculty of Louvain to establish an Index of prohibited books appropriate to the Netherlands. City magistrates who had been unwilling to execute heretics had fewer compunctions about prosecuting booksellers and seizing their wares. As in Italy, however, banned books continued to circulate surreptitiously.

At first the new religious policy appeared to succeed. There seem to have been about 30 executions for heresy prior to 1529, but this small total is misleading. Many leading Protestants took refuge in Germany where they formed churches in exile. Afterwards, convictions increased exponentially. The rise of millennial Anabaptism and the seizure of the north-German city of Münster by radicals, many of whom came from Holland, provoked a bloody repression after 1535. Horrified by reports of polygamy and communism among the Münsterites, magistrates cooperated with the government to an unprecedented degree. With the exception of a remnant salvaged by Menno Simons, the Anabaptist communities of the Low Countries were largely destroyed. In total, it has been estimated that the number of executions for heresy during the reign amounted to about 2000, most of them Anabaptists. Executions declined thereafter and virtually ceased in many regions during the 1550s. The decline was almost certainly due to a revival of magisterial independence. It is hard to believe that no unrepentant heretics could be found in Holland after 1553, but none were executed.

When Charles abdicated in 1555–56, the hated Anabaptists no longer posed a threat, but other forms of Protestantism survived. Throughout the reign, Protestants had found refuge in Antwerp and other major cities, as well as on the estates of sympathetic nobles. 'Lutheran' books, vernacular bibles, and other suspect literature remained available in spite of book burnings, and the exile churches in Germany stood ready to launch a new flood of activity when circumstances permitted. After 1559, the heretics grew bolder. In the early years of Philip II they sang and preached openly in public. Mobs sometimes forced the release of those arrested for heresy, and both the States of Brabant and the Flemish city of Bruges waged successful campaigns to keep the Inquisition at bay. Above all, the enthusiastic acceptance of Calvinism during the 1560s, especially in the south, casts doubt upon the success of Charles's religious policies. He contained heresy, but did not destroy it.

The religious issue symbolizes the Emperor's legacy in the Netherlands. He had expanded his holdings, ended the depredations of Gelre, and (Ghent aside) avoided open revolt. In nearly every other way he left fundamental problems that his son would find insoluble. The enormous cost of his wars, a burden shared fully by the Netherlands, made the regime unpopular and tied his hands in dealing with representative bodies. If anything, his policies inadvertently strengthened the provinces at the expense of the dynasty. Town governments and nobles alike remained as assertive at the end of the reign as they had been at the beginning, and on a number of occasions these normally hostile forces had worked together in unprecedented ways against the Emperor's own interests.

But Charles V did not precipitate the Revolt of the Netherlands. Though as much an absentee as his son, he avoided confrontation whenever possible and rarely if ever attempted to rule by fiat. He may not have been loved by his subjects, but as a Netherlander by birth and education, he was at least accepted by them as their natural prince. His son, Philip II, was Spanish to his fingertips, unpopular with his Netherlandish subjects, and heavy-handed in dealing with them. A more delicate touch might have avoided catastrophe, but even the most sensitive ruler would have needed luck as well. With the 17 provinces, Philip inherited unresolved issues of sovereignty, a cauldron of suppressed religious passions, and a massive Empire-wide debt that would hobble his policies at every level. The mixture exploded in little more than a decade.

5

THE SETTLEMENT OF EUROPE

Of the events and achievements that characterized the reign of Charles V, contemporaries were most impressed by the Emperor's decision to divide his possessions and abdicate his many titles while still in his mid-fifties. His action had few precedents, and few rulers have chosen to follow his example. We do not know with certainty when Charles first began to think about abdication, but the decision itself seems to have been reached at some point in 1553. His motives, though never fully explained, included his worsening physical ailments, and after the disasters of 1550–51, a growing battle with mental depression. He may also have wanted to ensure that what had become a very complicated succession would go smoothly, but this is doubtful. When Charles put aside his many offices and retired to the remote monastery of Yuste in Spanish Extremadura, he abandoned nearly all political activity. If his heirs hoped that he would help them in the transition – and there is no reason to suppose that they did – they would have been disappointed. Though Charles had no intention of becoming a monk, he was tired, disillusioned, and in his own mind, a failure. He wanted to be at peace and to prepare his soul for death in a location far from the struggles that had marked his career. Contemporaries saw in his retirement the humility and self-abnegation of a true Christian ruler. Their interpretation may have been partially true at best, but neither Charles nor his apologists saw fit to deny it.

Charles's personal feelings prompted him to abdicate. Politics and necessity determined the division of his Empire, but not before emotions of a different kind nearly derailed a process that had been in motion for decades. The disposition of the Emperor's vast inheritance had been at issue since before he attained his majority. Few believed that it would be possible to govern so many different realms effectively, and both Maximilian I and Ferdinand of Aragon had each proposed a division of responsibilities between Charles and his brother Ferdinand. Maximilian wanted Charles to rule Spain and Italy while Ferdinand would govern the German Empire, including the Netherlands. Ferdinand of Aragon proposed the opposite, in part because his namesake had been raised in Spain and was popular there, whereas Charles was a foreigner who knew nothing of the place or its language. In the end, both grandfathers withdrew their schemes before they died and left the brothers to negotiate a division of power among themselves. Charles, of course, inherited Spain and the Netherlands in his own name. The Austrian lands went to both of them jointly with Charles as the senior. Whatever Maximilian may have meant by this, it left Ferdinand with little more than a negotiating position based on the presumed love of a brother he scarcely knew and an unenforceable agreement that something, at least, ought to be done for him. Not surprisingly, a final settlement was reached only at the end of the reign. The process by which it was achieved combined paralyzing uncertainty, abrupt reversals of policy, and from Ferdinand's point of view, betrayal.

In 1520–21, after the imperial election, Charles gave Ferdinand the Austrian hereditary lands. During the crisis of 1523–25 he offered him the widely scattered territories of Milan, Pfirt, and Hainaut in return for his help. Ferdinand was not impressed. One of these states was in Italy, one in Germany, and the other in the southern Netherlands; none of them was firmly under Habsburg control. After the battle of Pavia, Charles reneged on even this meagre promise when it appeared for the first time that he might actually retain Milan. The Emperor was more helpful after Louis of Hungary died at Mohács in 1526. Charles helped to arrange Ferdinand's election as King of Hungary and Bohemia, titles which, though elective, would form the basis of a new Habsburg Empire in the east. Although he did little to assist him in his subsequent struggles against the Turks, Charles then played an important role in Ferdinand's election as King of the Romans in 1531. If he lived, this election guaranteed that Ferdinand would succeed his brother as Holy Roman Emperor. He assumed that as Emperor he could then arrange for his own heir to be elected King of the Romans in turn. For the remainder of the decade, it appeared that the division of the Empire proposed by Maximilian I would eventually come to pass, though not in Charles's lifetime.

As he approached his fortieth birthday, the Emperor began to think in broader terms about his legacy. In the next decade he would advance a variety of proposals that reflected the increasing volatility of his spirits in the face of triumphs and disappointments that followed one another in bewildering succession. The year 1539 was one of high hopes, if not euphoria. Buoyed by the prospect of a journey across France as the guest of Francis I and hopeful that the forthcoming Diet of Regensburg would resolve the religious issue in Germany, he began to think of new arrangements and alliances. Charles had married Isabella of Portugal in 1526. By her, he had three children: Philip (b. 1527), Mary (b. 1528), and Juana (b. 1535). Their interests had to be reconciled with those of his brother and his brother's heir, the future Maximilian II (b. 1527). At the same time, Charles had convinced himself that the long-term interests of the Habsburgs would best be served by a permanent alliance with the Valois dynasty of France, an alliance that would not only prevent future wars, but bind the two families into one great dynastic corporation that would rule all of Europe.

Charles's son Philip would rule Spain; on that point the Emperor never wavered. What other lands Philip might rule, however, remained an open question. Before Charles left on his campaign against Cleves and France in 1543 he appointed the 16-year-old Philip as Regent in Spain, leaving him with the first of his 'testaments,' a document filled with instructions and practical advice on the governance of Spain. At the same time, he raised the issue of how his empire was to be divided without resolving it. For some months he had engaged in correspondence with Ferdinand on just this issue, and knew that his brother still hoped for Milan, which he had been promised so many years before. Charles now suggested, among other dynastic possibilities, that perhaps his own daughter, Mary of Spain, should be given the Netherlands, while one of Ferdinand's daughters might have Milan. One of the two girls could then be married to the Duke of Orléans, son of Eleanor and Francis I.[1] This recipe for genetic disaster was the backdrop of the negotiations at Crépy in 1544. The treaty gave the Duke of Orléans his choice of either Charles's daughter Mary and the Netherlands or Ferdinand's daughter Anne and the Duchy of Milan, but the Emperor's undisguised relief at the death of Orléans indicates that he had changed his mind even before the treaty was signed. He had now decided that Philip should have the Netherlands as well as Spain.[2]

The inheritance issue became more heated after 1548. In that year, Mary of Spain, the older of the Emperor's daughters, married Ferdinand's eldest son, Maximilian. Her only dowry was a cash payment that Charles never paid in full. It was at this point that Charles severed the legal ties between his possessions in the Netherlands and the Holy Roman Empire and brought Philip from Spain to be named as his successor. Mary and Maximilian, who had wanted the Netherlands and were known to be angry over Philip's succession, would serve as Regents of Spain during Philip's absence without further compensation. Philip's visit to the Low Countries was not a success. He was now 21 and experienced in the uses of power. For five years he had governed the Spanish kingdoms with only sporadic interference from his father, and had already begun to demonstrate the prudence and conscientious attention to detail for which he would become famous. He was also reserved – almost shy – and ignorant of both French and Dutch. His new subjects thought him arrogant and realized that in cultural terms he was wholly Spanish and had little sympathy for their values. Though prepared to recognize him as the Emperor's legitimate heir, they did not like him. Philip, though he gained a thorough understanding of the region during his years in the Netherlands, appears to have reciprocated their dislike. This clash of personalities and cultures, never resolved, contributed greatly to the Revolt that began in 1566.[3]

Charles, meanwhile, seemed determined to do even more for Philip at the expense of Ferdinand and his heirs. The Emperor's health had deteriorated, and it may be that by this time he was already beginning to think about abdication. In 1550 he initiated talks with Ferdinand over the imperial succession. There were rumors that Maximilian planned to reunite the Netherlands with the Empire if he became Emperor, and that he might also choose to exercise his rights over the imperial fiefs in Italy, including Milan. Charles may have taken these adolescent fantasies seriously. In any case, he now suggested that Philip, not Maximilian, should succeed Ferdinand as King of the Romans. Maximilian could then succeed Philip in what Charles apparently hoped would be a regular rotation of the imperial office between the two branches of his family. Ferdinand and Maximilian were appalled. When Ferdinand did not immediately agree to this scheme, Charles met him at Augsburg where they were joined some months later by a desperate Maximilian. Both Ferdinand and his son saw this modification of the original agreement as a betrayal, and realized that if Charles had his way, Maximilian might not live to be Emperor. The argument became so heated that Mary of Hungary came to Augsburg to intervene on behalf of the Emperor. By the time the wrangling ended, the

Habsburg siblings were communicating only by letters carried from house to house by their servants. In the end, Ferdinand gave in, and the new agreement was published in March, 1551. When Charles died, Ferdinand would become Emperor, but would support Philip's candidacy as King of the Romans. When Philip in turn became Emperor, he would support the candidacy of Maximilian. Because both sides agreed that cooperation between the two branches of the family was essential, Philip would marry Maximilian's sister. Meanwhile, Philip and his heirs would rule the Netherlands and exercise imperial rights over the fiefs in Italy whenever the Emperor, be it Ferdinand or Maximilian, was not physically present.

In theory this bizarre arrangement preserved everyone's inheritance while guaranteeing that both sides of the family would be able to call upon the all-important resources of Spain in time of need. In reality its more important provisions were either unenforceable or unnecessary. If Charles believed that Maximilian might someday pose a threat to the Netherlands or Milan, he was mistaken. It was inconceivable that Maximilian could endanger any of Philip's possessions in the face of a Spanish army. Moreover, Ferdinand and Maximilian had accepted the agreement under duress, and if Ferdinand's patience was nearly endless, his son's was not. Maximilian began negotiations with the Electors on his own behalf almost before the ink on the agreement of 1551 was dry. Charles knew this, and advanced a strange scheme to have Philip elected immediately as a second King of the Romans in addition to Ferdinand. Ferdinand and the Electors refused to accept this violation of imperial custom, but by this time the absurdity of the Emperor's plans for his succession had become obvious. The Electors of the Empire were unlikely to support Philip's candidacy under any circumstances. In 1555, the year of his father's abdication, Philip had the good sense to renounce his claim as King of the Romans. Maximilian followed Ferdinand as King of the Romans and then Holy Roman Emperor, while Philip went on to rule Spain, the Netherlands, and Italy as originally planned.

This episode, which strained the unity of the Habsburgs to its limit, arose from the Emperor's growing conviction that only Spanish resources could preserve his inheritance. That belief may have prompted his effort to secure the imperial inheritance for Philip. It was certainly the reason that he decided to give the Netherlands to Philip rather than keeping it within the Holy Roman Empire. Over the years Charles had become more dependent upon his Spanish possessions. They alone could be counted upon to bolster the vast structure he had inherited, and only they would oppose the inroads of heresy without hesitation. By 1545 his chief financial adviser, his leading general, and even his confessor were Spanish. Most of the funds used for campaigns outside the Netherlands came from Castilian taxpayers, supplemented by occasional windfalls from the Spanish Indies. The Spanish *tercios* remained the core of his armies, an elite force upon which he could rely even in the most desperate circumstances. Now grown comfortable with the Spanish language and culture, Charles had come to think of Castile as the keystone of his Empire and he must have doubted that any part of it could long endure without Spanish support.

The Emperor's flight to Innsbruck in 1552, where he had to be rescued by Spanish and Italian troops, strengthened this conviction. Continuing French hostility sealed it. After his successful defense of Metz, Henry II reopened the war on two fronts. In 1553 a combined French, Ottoman, and North African fleet seized Corsica from the Genoese. Though money remained in desperately short supply, Philip and his father found the means to assist Doria's attempted recovery of the island in 1554. In the Low Countries, Henry II launched new assaults in both 1553 and 1554, harrying Artois and Hainaut and threatening the heartland of Brabant. This new invasion after years of warfare left the Netherlands financially and militarily exhausted. Both Charles and his sister, Mary of Hungary, realized that even with its enormous wealth, the country might not always be defensible without access to Spanish money and Spanish arms. As part of Ferdinand's ramshackle empire it would surely be lost. In their hearts they feared that even the wealth and power of Spain might not be enough.

Worry over the Netherlands and the failure of his scheme to alter the imperial succession encouraged Charles to reconsider his dynastic options. The year 1553 was a miserable one. After Metz, Charles retired to Brussels where he spent months tormented by gout, hemorrhoids, and other ailments that were aggravated by the cold and by his usual rich diet. Mary continued to govern the Netherlands as if he were not there. For a time he sank into profound depression, locking himself in his apartments and refusing to see anyone. It was reported that he wept constantly like a child, and his doctors thought that he could not live much longer. In his own mind, abdication was now certain.

The following year brought little improvement in the Emperor's condition, but a new dynastic opportunity had presented itself. The Protestant King Edward VI of England died in July, 1553, at the age of 15, leaving the throne to his Catholic sister Mary. The wars with France might never end, but if England were bound by marriage to Spain and the Netherlands, French ambitions in northwest Europe could perhaps be neutralized. Philip at the moment remained unmarried, though he had begun negotiations for the hand of Maria of Portugal, apparently on his own initiative. Close ties between the Iberian powers had always been a cornerstone of Habsburg marital strategy. Philip was himself the product of the Emperor's union with a Portuguese princess, and Philip's first wife, another Maria, had been Portuguese as well.[4] She died in 1545 giving birth to Philip's son, the unfortunate Don Carlos, who would succumb to madness and die prematurely in 1568. For eight years Philip had enjoyed his role as Europe's most eligible batchelor. Now, the possibility of incorporating England into the Habsburg system proved more attractive than further ties to Portugal. The Portuguese negotiations were allowed to cool. Charles roused himself from lethargy long enough to authorize Cardinal Granvelle and his ambassador Simon Renard to begin negotiations with England.

Their task proved unexpectedly easy. Mary Tudor, anxious to preserve her throne and restore the Catholic faith, agreed to the Spanish marriage in the face of strong objections from her Council. Philip set sail for England with a large entourage, leaving the government of Spain in the hands of his sister Juana. Their wedding took place on 25 July, 1554. On the preceding day, Philip learned that his father had abdicated Naples and Milan in his favor. As King of Naples, Philip would be a king in his own right and theoretically equal to his bride in prestige. As King of England his powers were strictly limited. In an arrangement that resembled the one concluded by Ferdinand and Isabella so many years before, Philip would share all titles and responsibilities with the Queen, appoint no foreigners to any kind of office, and relinquish his title if Mary should die before him. Their heirs, if any, would inherit the throne. Philip accepted these limitations with good grace, and behaved with circumspection when in England, but he could not earn the trust of the English. They disliked his Spanish retinue, whose members disliked them in return, and feared that England would be drawn into the interminable disputes of the Continent.

The marriage of Philip and Mary produced two false pregnancies but no children, and ended with Mary's death in 1558. The vision of England as a counterweight to French power in the north died with her, though Philip tried to keep it alive even after Elizabeth I ascended the English throne and reimposed Protestantism. By this time the Emperor was long dead. The story of how England and Spain became mortal enemies belongs to the reign of Philip II. While Charles and Mary lived, the English alliance remained in effect, but the vigilant hostility of Mary's ministers rendered it useless in military terms. England would contribute neither men, money, nor credit to the Habsburg cause.

Meanwhile, the Emperor had begun to divest himself of his remaining titles. On 22 October, 1555, he resigned as Master of the Order of the Golden Fleece. Three days later, in a moving ceremony at Brussels, he abdicated as ruler of the Netherlands in favor of his son Philip. Dressed in mourning and leaning on the shoulder of Prince William of Orange, the young man who would one day lead the Revolt of the Netherlands against Philip, Charles renounced his offices, asking the forgiveness of all present. He then collapsed in his chair amid universal weeping. His sister, Mary of Hungary, resigned at the same time, to be replaced as Regent by Emmanuele Filiberto of Savoy. At the request of his brother Ferdinand, Charles retained the imperial title but made it clear that he had no further intention of exercising whatever authority it conferred. In the following year, Charles bestowed his Spanish kingdoms and the Franche-Comté on Philip and abdicated as Emperor, leaving Ferdinand to be elected in his place. The final transfer of power did not take place, however, until February, 1558. A small, but luxurious villa had been prepared for him in the grounds of the Jeronimite monastery of Yuste in Extremadura where he now intended to retire, but there was no money available to finance the journey. After delays that must have seemed interminable, Charles of Habsburg set sail at last for Spain in September, 1557.

During this confused period of transition, Philip emerged as an effective ruler. Though father and son disagreed on a number of issues, imperial forces and their allies nevertheless made headway against the French. Siena fell in 1554, and it was Philip who engineered the settlement by which he became the city's Vicar and then subinfeudated it to Cosimo of Florence. In 1556–57 the reforming Pope Paul IV imprudently allied himself with the French and threatened the Neapolitan marches. Willful and choleric, he hated the imperialists and hoped to drive them from the peninsula for reasons that had more to do with the politics of his native Naples than with the interests of the Holy See. Philip, who if anything was more devoutly Catholic than his father, had no desire to quarrel with the Pope who had restored the Roman Inquisition and devised the *Index Librorum Prohibitorum*, but a series of outrageous incidents left him little choice. An army under the Duke of Alba forced the French to retreat. Then, with consummate delicacy, Alba placed his troops before the poorly defended walls of Rome and negotiated a settlement through intermediaries in the College of Cardinals.

Before the scandal of a war between the two foremost champions of the Catholic Reformation could be brought to an end, Henry II reopened the war in the north by attacking Douai while reviving the Scottish alliance in an attempt to neutralize England. Philip, now back in the Netherlands, directed the course of the subsequent campaign, but did not participate in the final battle. On 10 August, 1557, Emmanuele Filiberto of Savoy, the new Regent of the Netherlands, destroyed a large French army near the village of St Quentin on the main road between Brussels and Paris. Paris was now open to attack as it had been in 1543, but like Charles before him, Philip lacked the resources to pursue his advantage. In 1558 Henry II retaliated by seizing Calais from the English. The loss of England's last possession in France had great symbolic importance, but both combatants were now at the edge of financial ruin. Philip had repudiated his debts in 1557; Henry II followed in 1558. Mary of England died in November of the same year, ending whatever hopes Philip may still have entertained about English assistance. With both France and Spain now officially bankrupt, the Habsburg–Valois rivalry ground at last to its inglorious end. By the Treaty of Câteau-Cambrésis (3 April, 1559), France kept Calais but gave up most of Savoy, which returned to the victorious Emanuele Filiberto.

To seal the agreement the newly bereft Philip married Henry II's eldest daughter Elizabeth of Valois in a ceremony performed by proxy on 22 June, 1559. The festivities, which lasted for days, included a tournament during which the 40-year-old Henry insisted on running a final course against a much younger opponent. The man's lance broke and entered the King's visor, piercing his eye and entering the brain. Henry remained lucid enough to create a regency government for his sickly 15-year-old son, Francis II, before dying at last on 10 July. The regency marked the beginning of more than 30 years of turmoil, known with pardonable oversimplification as the Wars of Religion. France would pose no major threat to Philip II for the remainder of his reign.

Charles did not live to see the Treaty of Câteau-Cambrésis. To the final struggles of the war against France he had contributed little beyond pressing his daughter Juana to send more money to Philip in her capacity as Regent of Spain. The great struggle with France, to which he had devoted much of his life, ended without him.

The struggle with the German princes also ended without his active participation. After the agreement at Passau, Charles left Germany knowing that the upcoming Diet of Augsburg in 1555 would resolve the problems of Germany with a compromise. The knowledge that this agreement would effectively recognize the Lutherans and invalidate most of the policies he had pursued over more than 30 years contributed greatly to his depression. In June of 1554 he asked his brother Ferdinand to preside over the Diet and conduct the negotiations as King of the Romans, 'acting neither in my name nor by grant of any special powers from me.'[5] Charles was at this point physically and emotionally incapable of dealing with the princes. Wounded in pride and conscience, he simply could not bring himself to attend the Diet, and would have preferred to abdicate his imperial title rather than do so. Ferdinand agreed to preside, but insisted that Charles remain Emperor and endorse the final agreement *in absentia*. Neither of the brothers wished to accept blame for what they knew would be a disagreeable outcome.

The Peace of Augsburg held few surprises. The Diet agreed on the basic principle later described as *cuius regio, eius religio*. A prince, in other words, had the right to determine the religion of his subjects as long as that religion was Catholic or Lutheran. Other faiths would not be tolerated. Imperial cities that were now exclusively Lutheran or Catholic would remain so, but the eight cities that were currently divided on confessional lines would have to tolerate both Catholics and Lutherans equally. To protect Lutheran interests, church property secularized before 1552 would remain 'territorial church land' under the authority of the ruling prince or city government that held them, but no further secularizations would be permitted. To protect the Catholics, it was decreed that if a prince-bishop or prince-abbott decided to become a Lutheran, he would have to resign in favor of a Catholic. This 'ecclesiastical reservation' was proclaimed by authority of the Emperor. It was never voted on by the Diet or approved by the Protestants, and would become a source of conflict in the years to come.

Another source of controversy was a secret agreement called the *Declaratio Ferdinandei*. In discussions before the Diet, Ferdinand had agreed that if towns or noblemen under the jurisdiction of an ecclesiastical prince had been practicing Lutheranism for a period of years, they would be allowed to continue. When the contents of the *Declaratio* were revealed 20 years later, some of the bishops predictably rejected it as a fraud. The question of imperial organization was addressed in the Diet's Recess by an 'Executive Ordinance' giving the Imperial Circles (*Kreise*) the power to administer law and order and to execute the decisions of the *Reichskammergericht*. This actually weakened imperial authority because the *Reichskammergericht* and several of the *Kreise* were by this time controlled by the princes. Other circles, like that of Swabia, were paralyzed by political and confessional divisions too bewildering to describe here. The settlement reached at Augsburg would remain the basis of political life in the Holy Roman Empire until the outbreak of the Thirty Years' War. Imperial authority remained weak, and would grow weaker when Ferdinand divided his estates among his heirs instead of leaving them all to his succesor, Maximilian II. This division of the Habsburg lands proved temporary, but under the reclusive Rudolph II (d. 1612), the Emperor's influence declined again to be revived during the Thirty Years' War by Ferdinand II. Meanwhile, the power of the princes continued to grow.

Without a strong Emperor, the religious settlement proved unenforceable. The Pope never accepted the Augsburg agreement, though he permitted Catholics to observe it until better circumstances permitted them to renew the struggle. The Protestants were no happier. Having signed the ecclesiastical reservation under protest, many of them felt free to ignore it and continued to secularize church property. In the eight towns that were ordered to tolerate both faiths Catholics were actively, if unofficially, persecuted by the Protestant majority. Confessional differences hardened as the century advanced. Catholics, in particular, were emboldened by the final condemnation of Protestant doctrines by the Council of Trent in 1563 and by the growing success of the Counter-Reformation. This movement, which reclaimed large areas of Germany in the second half of the century, was inspired less by popes and emperors than by the Catholic princes who supported Jesuit missions and encouraged their bishops to implement the decrees of Trent. The reconversions came largely at the expense of Lutheranism, which was at this time bitterly divided between Gnesio-Lutherans, who would not modify the teachings of Luther, and the Philippists, who accepted the views of Luther's colleague Melanchthon. Outbreaks of confessional violence grew as it became obvious that neither the Emperor nor the hopelessly divided Diet could enforce religious peace.

A more serious flaw in the agreement became obvious on the day after the Diet of Augsburg adjourned. The Elector Frederick III of the Palatinate announced that he had become a Calvinist. John Calvin, the reformer of Geneva, held views on the sacraments and on other matters that were as repugnant to many Lutherans as they were to Catholics. In 1555 Calvin's followers had been few, and were excluded, like other branches of the Reformed tradition, from the settlement at Augsburg. Their numbers increased as the Calvinist movement became popular in Bohemia and Hungary, and was reinforced in Germany by the defection of Philippists after the Lutheran state churches adopted the Gnesio-Lutheran Formula of Concord between 1577 and 1580. In 1613 the Elector of Brandenburg converted, leaving the Empire with two Calvinist Electors out of seven. As neither they nor any of the smaller states that had adopted Calvinism enjoyed the protection of imperial law, they tended to seek alliances outside the Empire, thereby adding to the tensions that created the Thirty Years' War. Charles V, of course, had known that the Peace of Augsburg would settle nothing. It represented the defeat of his German policy, and he sought to disassociate himself from it from the beginning. But what of the other arrangements by which he had hoped to secure the future of his dynasty?

The centerpiece of the plan, the division of his Empire, was probably unavoidable. Charles had promised the imperial title to Ferdinand at the beginning of the reign because he needed his brother's help in managing German affairs. Subsequent events proved the wisdom of that decision. The task of defending Charles's inheritance was beyond the capacity of one individual and could barely be managed by all of the Habsburgs together. The family quarrel that followed in 1551 was nevertheless a mistake that, like the decision to attack Metz, reveals the Emperor's judgment to have been clouded by adversity. The squabble over the inheritance changed nothing and might have led to a serious breech between the two branches of the family had not Ferdinand once again displayed an almost saintly forbearance. After Philip, with equal forbearance, renounced the agreement of 1551, relations between the Spanish and Austrian Habsburgs became friendlier than Charles had any reason to expect. Though Philip and Ferdinand disagreed over the imperial vicarate in northern Italy, they generally supported each other's policies and avoided controversy until the accession of Maximilian II in 1564. The alliance lapsed after Maximilian and his sons, Matthias and Rudolph II, offered diplomatic support to the Netherlandish rebels and was not restored until after Rudolph's death in 1612. Thereafter, Habsburg cooperation would play an important role in the Thirty Years' War.

Charles, however, was now beyond such concerns. When he retired to the monastery at Yuste, he ceased as far as possible to interfere with the business of government. His sisters Eleanor and Mary came to visit, and his illegitimate son Don Juan of Austria, already handsome and charming at the age of ten came to live nearby, though until this point Charles had barely acknowledged his existence. Juana and Philip importuned him on occasion for advice, but for the most part the last year of his life was free from the stresses of war and politics. He had a few books and the company of his confessor, together with a household of about 50 whom he supported on an annual pension of 20 000 ducats. No ascetic, Charles nevertheless attended Mass regularly in the chapel of the Jeronimite monks, which was connected to his villa by a covered walkway, and pursued a daily routine based in large part on prayer and contemplation. Much of the time he spent in the sun on his terrace overlooking the beautiful valley of the Vera. His wish to put the great world behind him was nothing if not genuine. In August, 1558, he contracted a fever of uncertain origin. His doctors, as usual, attributed it to overindulgence in venison and anchovies, but could do nothing for him. Charles of Habsburg, once ruler of much of the known world, died quietly on 21 September. His sister and perhaps the greatest of his servants, Mary of Hungary followed him to the grave in November.

6

THE REIGN OF CHARLES V
IN HISTORY

The reign of Charles V was a pivotal era in the world's history. Spiritually and intellectually, Europe transformed itself. The Reformation shattered a millennium and a half of religious unity. New forms of religious life arose while older ideas began to acquire new vigor as the Catholic Church reformed itself from within. Meanwhile, the Renaissance as an intellectual movement lost much of its impetus and creativity, though its influence on taste and scholarship remained intact.

Politically, the Emperor's Spanish subjects conquered Mexico and Peru and laid the foundation of a worldwide Spanish empire. By so doing, they advanced the growth of a world market, not merely because they opened new continents for exploitation, but because their conquests provided much-needed specie for the commercial expansion of other nations in Africa and Asia. In time, bullion from the New World would have an augmentative effect on European warfare. In the meantime, the long series of wars between Charles V and France culminated in Spanish domination of the Italian peninsula. In eastern Europe the Habsburgs blocked Ottoman expansion in the Danube valley and created a multinational empire that lasted until 1918. Germany alone seemed to continue on its old political course in all but religion, a confederation of independent cities and princely states bound loosely together by the institutions of the medieval Empire. In all of these realms institutional and political arrangements assumed the general outlines they would retain until the end of the Old Regime. Even in the Netherlands, which the Emperor's dynastic policy tied to Spain with disasterous and unforeseen results, his government created or modified institutions that would survive in both the Spanish Netherlands and the Dutch Republic.

Inspired by the importance of these developments, historians have studied Charles V and his age for more than four centuries. They have achieved general agreement on questions of fact, but their interpretations of his life and reign vary. In the Emperor's lifetime and for many years thereafter, historical assessments of the age were colored by a favorable view of Charles V as a ruler and as a person. This was, in part, because he was genuinely admired in his own time. It was also because, like most rulers, the Emperor cultivated his public image with great care, and his immediate successors, whose own power rested in large part on the arrangements he had made, made every effort to preserve his reputation. Historians of the sixteenth and seventeenth centuries therefore tended to see him as a model ruler: prudent, dignified, and conscientious. Even his abdication and retirement to a monastery was seen as evidence of a Christian humility that stood in marked contrast to the pride and worldliness of Francis I and Henry VIII. If the Emperor failed in many of his enterprises, early writers thought that it was largely owing to circumstances beyond his control. True, his judgment was sometimes faulty, but neither he nor anyone else possessed the means to turn back the tides of religious change while simultaneously fighting the French and Turks.

This generous view prevailed until the end of the eighteenth-century Enlightenment, though by that time most of the writers who held it were not in any sense sympathetic to Charles's religious conservativism. Since then, the Emperor's personal reputation has suffered from the scrutiny of a less forgiving age. The realization that his retirement was not monkish, that he had the normal human complement of human vices, and that he was at times subject to something like mental illness has reduced his figure, perhaps unfairly, to more human proportions. His reign, too, has been re-examined from different and less flattering perspectives, many of them based on moral or political values wholly alien to Charles and the age in which he lived.

Modern assessments of the reign of Charles V begin with Leopold von Ranke (1795–1888). Few scholars have had a comparable impact on the development of history as a discipine. During his long career at the University of Berlin, Ranke insisted on the critical examination of archival sources as the basis of political and military history. His rigorous analysis of historical documents owed a great, if largely unacknowledged, debt to the older disciplines of linguistics and philology, but his application of those methods to the writing of history, his shrewd understanding of men and sources, and his eloquent German style made him the first, and perhaps the greatest, of modern historians. He was also the most influential of educators. His seminars formed nearly all of the leading German historians of the nineteenth and early twentieth centuries, and through them his influence extended to England and the United States.

Ranke's great interest was in the political and military history of the Renaissance and Reformation. He believed, like the historians of the Enlightenment before him, that the fifteenth and sixteenth centuries marked the beginnings of the modern state. The reign of Charles V was therefore of critical importance because it explained, among other things, why Germany had not evolved into a monarchy like those of western Europe. The Emperor's inability either to accept or to destroy the Protestant Reformation allowed the Holy Roman Empire to remain a relic of the Middle Ages, a loose federation of cities and principalities incompatible with the development of nationhood. Ranke, who was both a German nationalist and a Protestant, viewed this development with profound ambivalence. He saw the survival of Protestantism as an essential component of human progress, but believed that the Germans as a people could not realize their fullest potential without a unified state. Meanwhile, the Habsburgs, frustrated in Germany, turned to the east and Austria, too, evolved into a multinational empire of a kind wholly unlike the states of western Europe.

Ranke believed that Charles lacked the resources to match his goals, but he also thought that the Emperor was to some extent an anachronism, a medieval figure whose dreams of universal empire prevented him from grasping the crucial moment in German history. Instead of trying to forge the Holy Roman Empire into a German monarchy, Charles created a worldwide empire based on Spain. This decision was disastrous for Germany, which remained weak and divided until the unification movement of Ranke's own time, but it was worse for Spain, which did not possess the wealth and manpower to meet its new responsibilities. Above all, by separating the Low Countries from their historic roots in the Empire and granting them to Philip II, Charles created an unnatural situation that paved the way for the Revolt of the Netherlands. The Dutch finally achieved their independence after a long and bitter struggle, though the southern provinces did not, but Spain, unable to preserve its hold on the Low Countries while maintaining its other worldwide commitments, sank into decline together with its Italian subject states.

Few today would quarrel with the facts that underlie this statement. After Charles V, the Empire remained the same loose federation of states that it had always been. Protestantism survived, though it did not triumph, and the Habsburgs developed a multinational empire of their own in eastern Europe that bore little resemblance to the political structures of the west. The Netherlands rebelled under Charles's successor, and Spain entered on a long period of political and economic decline, albeit after a century of something very like hegemony in Europe. But if the facts themselves are unquestioned, the value judgments in which Ranke and his many followers immersed them have been challenged by more recent historians in Germany and elsewhere. The idea that the development of monarchies on the French, Spanish, or English models was somehow the norm, and that the rest of Europe was therefore an aberration has become as difficult to sustain as the related notion that the self-realization of a people is always dependent upon being organized into a nation state with a common culture and centralized political institutions.

Gerald Strauss, Thomas A. Brady, Heinz Schilling, and Volker Press, among others, have argued that what came to be called the Holy Roman Empire of the German nation was both natural and an effective adaptation to German conditions. Charles V would have agreed. The legal and constitutional status of the German princes was far different from that of 'overmighty subjects' in England, France, or Spain, and German cities likewise enjoyed a degree of freedom unknown in those countries. In the absence of an outside power capable of posing a credible threat to German security, there could be no basis for the kind of monarchy that evolved in the west. Charles V, of course, never attempted to create one. His goals in Germany were far more practical. On the rare occasions when Charles sought to tinker with the imperial constitution, it was to develop more effective means for adjudicating disputes between the states or for the development of a common foreign policy on such issues as Ottoman expansion. He did not want a different kind of Germany, but hoped only for one that might be slightly less dysfunctional. That the Emperor failed to achieve even this modest goal was due only in part to the Reformation. Religious issues made compromise and even negotiation more difficult, but the reform of imperial institutions would have been difficult in any case. There was simply no incentive to tinker with a system that seemed to benefit cities and princes alike. The failure of the Protestant League of Schmalkalden to develop an effective system of internal governance demonstrates that the problem of German unity was not primarily religious but political.

But if the Reformation did not in itself set Germany on a course different from that of the western monarchies, it was by far the most important development of the reign. Charles himself was painfully aware that under his rule the religious unity of Latin Christendom had shattered, perhaps forever. His failure either to suppress the Reformation or to compromise with it was the greatest of his disappointments and a contributing factor in the mental depression that engulfed his later years. But what, in hindsight, could he have done differently?

Compromise was almost certainly out of the question. The Reformation involved profound differences over faith and religious practice. The Colloquy of Regensburg showed that men of good will might come close to bridging the gap on justification only to have compromise flatly rejected by their backers. On the sacraments, and above all, on papal authority, there could never be agreement. The question of authority touched the self-interest of princes and city governments who profited enormously from controlling their own churches, while no pope could for a moment consider what amounted to an abdication of his divinely established authority. This, even more than private interest and transient political calculations, forced Clement VII and Paul III to obstruct Charles in his desire for a general council. A council that diminished papal authority was unacceptable; a council that did not would never be accepted by the Protestants.

Attempting to suppress the Reformation by force worked no better than compromise. Charles could impose Catholic orthodoxy in his own hereditary lands, often with considerable difficulty, but he was almost powerless to do so outside them. In Germany, even military victory against the Protestants could not force them in the long run to modify their beliefs. The aftermath of the Schmalkaldic wars demonstrated that Charles could for a time enforce his religious policy by imposing a military occupation on parts of the German southwest, but even there the Protestants showed themselves experts at evasion and passive resistance. In the Protestant north and east the princely states were too large and well-armed to be occupied. When the princes attacked him in 1550–51, only four years after their defeat in the Schmalkaldic wars, Charles learned that they could not even be neutralized. His resources were great, but not great enough to reimpose Catholicism on the sovereign states of the Empire if they were determined to resist him.

The only alternative to force or compromise would have been to accept Protestantism himself. This, of course, he could not do for obvious reasons. Personal conviction and the nature of the imperial office aside, Charles would not have sacrificed his hereditary lands in Spain, Italy, and the Netherlands to pursue the chimera of a unified German Protestant state. It was a notion that never occurred to him or to any of his contemporaries. Had he done so, there is no guarantee that the Catholic princes, a majority of whom were bishops, would have followed him, or that the Protestants would have abandoned their cherished political autonomy. In short, it is almost inconceivable that the Emperor could have followed a different German policy, or that any other policy would have produced significantly different results. The reign of Charles V will always be known as the age of the Reformation, but the movement itself was too complex and powerful to be controlled by him or by any other individual.

The division of his Empire and the creation of a Habsburg polity based on central and eastern Europe was another consequence of the reign that has been seen as a turning point in European history. The reasons for the division need not be repeated, but did Charles divide his Empire in the best possible way? The question forces us to indulge in the speculative and unhistorical game of 'counterfactual conditionals,' but in this case there is no alternative. We cannot understand the legacy of Charles V without looking at what might have happened had he chosen to act differently.

In retrospect, the decision to tie Italy to Spain was correct, strategically and culturally. Charles could not, in any case, have ignored the historic relationship between Aragon, Naples, Sicily, and Sardinia, while Milan and the elaborate system of clientage he had developed in northern Italy could never have been protected by the Austrian Habsburgs. Italian patriots might have preferred a different solution, but in the sixteenth century and for centuries thereafter no Italian state was capable of serving as the nucleus of a free Italy. The choice was domination by either Spain or France. Croce and others blamed the subsequent woes of Italy on the economic backwardness of Spain, but they knew from historical experience that French rule might have been worse.

Tying the Netherlands to Spain, however, has been generally condemned. By 1572, the Low Countries were in full rebellion against Philip II. By 1589, Spanish arms and diplomacy had recaptured the ten southern provinces, but the north achieved full independence after nearly 80 years of warfare. As the United Provinces of the Netherlands, or Dutch Republic, it embarked upon a golden age that lasted for most of the seventeenth century. For Spain, the revolt provoked conflicts with England and France and imposed economic burdens that became unbearable. The Spanish system of finance, another legacy of Charles V, broke down, and by 1648 France replaced Spain as the dominant power in Europe. Spanish historians, writing from a national point of view, have claimed that the Emperor dragged their country into European responsibilities with disastrous results. Dutch historians have deplored 80 years of needless bloodshed.

These criticisms are based on the assumption that when Charles left the 17 provinces of the Low Countries to Philip as King of Spain, the Revolt of the Netherlands became inevitable. This viewpoint, best illustrated in the works of Pieter Geyl, is based in part on the nationalist assumption that the culture of the Netherlands was incompatible with that of Spain and that two such diverse cultures could not function under the same monarchy. Another, less ideological, argument supports the view of Alba and Charles's other Spanish advisers who said at the time of Crépy that the Netherlands was indefensible. Neither viewpoint is necessarily correct.

Arguments based on national culture are questionable for several reasons. Geyl's vision of a 'Netherlandish' culture in the sixteenth century has been questioned, as he knew it would be, by those who point to the region's extreme linguistic and institutional diversity. Moreover, there is little evidence of fundamental conflict between Spanish residents of the Netherlands and their hosts until the reign of Philip II. Spanish merchants had lived and worked without friction in Antwerp for decades and at Bruges for generations. Religious differences between Spanish Catholics and the Catholics of the Netherlands were probably no greater than those found among Catholics today. Netherlanders in the reign of Charles V sometimes resented his government for its exactions and for its occasional failure to protect them, but there is little evidence that they thought of it as culturally alien. Put simply, Charles did not anticipate the Revolt of the Netherlands because the provinces were firmly under control throughout his reign. The Revolt was provoked by Philip II, not his father, and it is impossible to predict what might have happened had Philip possessed his father's political skill and understanding of his Netherlandish possessions.

The argument that Spain was incapabable of defending the Netherlands is equally questionable, based as it is on a misunderstanding of Alba's position in 1544. The Duke argued against the abandonment of Milan because he saw it as the strategic heart of the empire. Neither the Netherlands, nor Spain's position in the Mediterranean could be maintained without it, and it was therefore better, if a choice had to be made, to give up the Netherlands rather than Milan. Charles, of course, could no more have anticipated the collapse of French power after 1559 than he could predict the coming of the Netherlands Revolt. The absence of a credible French threat helped Philip greatly in his war with the rebels, but it is worth noting that the Netherlands proved anything but indefensible. As we have seen, armies paid for and organized by Spain not only regained the ten southern provinces, but managed to carry on the fight against the north for nearly 80 years. During that time Spain also fought naval wars against England and the Turks, and in the 1590s invaded France. The Emperor's arrangements may not have been as foolish as they have sometimes seemed.

It is also permissable to think about what might have happened if the Netherlands had been given to Ferdinand and Maximilian. It is doubtful that the Austrian Habsburgs would have insisted on political or religious reforms of the kind imposed by Philip II. Lacking a serious threat to their privileges, the Netherlands might well have remained peacefully within the Empire until France recovered from its own civil wars and resumed its traditional policies. What might have happened then is anyone's guess, though the wars of Louis XIV provide some useful clues. The other possibility is that the Netherlands, already conscious of their own identity and largely indifferent to the Empire, might at some point have declared independence anyway. The Austrians would have been unable to stop such a movement, but their very weakness would have precluded anything like the bloody, 80-year struggle against Spain. From a Netherlandish, non-Habsburg perspective it is obvious that either outcome would have been preferrable to what actually happened.

But if Charles's crystal ball was as cloudy as our own, could he have done more to prepare his son for the tasks ahead of him? The answer is probably not. Few princes have been better trained or more experienced when they came to the throne. It is hard to imagine a more conscientious, knowledgeable, or well-informed ruler. Philip II had serious faults, but they could not in all probabilty have been eradicated by mere education: an infuriating tendency to micromanage and a perversely inept grasp of public relations, encouraged perhaps by his preference for working in relative isolation. It is perhaps more useful to ask if Philip's policies were those that would have been pursued by Charles V.

Philip's veneration for his deceased father was legendary. The two men shared a deep attachment to the Catholic faith and the determination, reinforced in Philip's case by his father's repeated injunctions, to give up not one inch of the family's inheritance. Charles had also thought that the Church in the Netherlands needed reform, and that the entire country would benefit from a uniform code of laws. Philip may therefore have believed that he was continuing in his father's footsteps when, in the 1560s, he began to refashion the Church, the legal system, and the governing councils of the Netherlands. But whenever Charles, in any of his realms, had embarked on the perilous course of institutional reform he had done so incrementally and with great delicacy, listening at all times to the views of his subjects. Above all, and especially in the Netherlands, he had protected the interests of the great nobles and catered to their vanity.

Philip behaved differently. He reduced the number of nobles on the Councils of State, Justice, and Finance, and appointed Cardinal Granvelle, a commoner who was not of Netherlandish descent, to the Presidency of the Council of State. This office had traditionally been held by a prominent member of the old Burgundian nobility. The King then proposed legal reforms that would, among other things, abolish manorial courts, an important source of noble revenues. Even the papal bull of 1559 that expanded the number of bishropics in the Low Countries from three to 14 contained a provision that all candidates for ecclesiastical office be of high moral character and trained in either theology or canon law. This, in effect, excluded the younger sons of the nobility and made it far more difficult for their families to provide for them. When Philip refused to modify his policies in the face of noble protests, he destroyed the ancient alliance between his dynasty and the Burgundian aristocracy. Other groups, including Protestants and the many defenders of local privilege and tradition grew equally disaffected, but it was the moral and material support of the Prince of Orange and many of his fellow aristocrats that proved critical in the early years of the Revolt. It is hard to imagine that Charles, who had so carefully cultivated a relationship with his fellow Knights of the Golden Fleece, would have allowed matters to reach this point.

The Revolt of the Netherlands, in other words, might have been avoided unless one assumes that multinational empires are inherently unworkable. This was, of course, the viewpoint of nationalist historians who have been equally critical of the empire created by the Austrian Habsburgs in central Europe. To them, the Austrian Empire inhibited the development of its component parts by denying expression to national aspirations that barely existed in the reign of Charles V. To others, the survival of the Austrian Empire for more than 300 years indicates that it was not unnatural, but a polity uniquely suited to a region of many peoples, none of whom were numerous enough or wealthy enough to survive individually in the face of Ottoman expansion, or, as they have since demonstrated, to live in peace with their neighbours.

These political assessments of the reign of Charles V rest, like all other judgements in history, on the judge's own values and ideological presuppositions. Those who accept nationalism as inevitable or good will disagree with those who believe that it was neither. Assessments of the intellectual and cultural impact of the reign, though based largely on religious rather than political values, have been equally divided. Catholics and Protestants have held different views on the Reformation and how it developed, though the two historiographic traditions are now growing closer together. A more complex dispute involves the perception, still widespread among students of history, that the reign of Charles V marked the end of the Renaissance.

The Renaissance, in this case, refers not to a historical period whose limits are arbitrary at best, but to an intellectual movement that, beginning in the mid-fourteenth century, sought to revive interest in the classics of ancient Greece and Rome. In the time of Charles V the scholars who pursued these interests came to be called humanists because they studied humane or secular literature. Two centuries later the savants of the Enlightenment saw in this Renaissance humanism a precursor of their own rationalist and anti-clerical concerns. By reviving the study of classical antiquity and attacking scholasticism the humanists had, in their view, dealt a powerful blow to medieval ignorance and superstition and begun the process that in their own time had led to a more rational and scientific approach to human affairs.

The great Swiss historian Jacob Burckhardt, a pupil and critic of Ranke, presented a richer, more nuanced interpretation in his *Civilization of the Renaissance in Italy* (1860). Though the Renaissance represented many things, it marked above all 'the discovery of the world and of man,' or the beginnings of a predominantly secular worldview. To the majority of historians who accepted one version or another of this view during the late nineteenth and early twentieth century, the Renaissance therefore possessed an important component of rational, secular ideology. A corollary held that the 'Counter-Reformation,' beginning with the Council of Trent and the revitalization of the Papal Inquisition in the time of Charles V, destroyed the Renaissance as a movement by persecuting its exponents.

Since the 1950s this idea has been attacked on several fronts. P. O. Kristeller's suggestion that Renaissance humanism had no ideological basis beyond the desire to study the classics and apply them to the present has been widely accepted. Even those who reject such a minimalist definition agree that the movement was anything but monolithic. Humanists shared a common method and set of interests, but could be found on different sides of almost every issue. Case-by-case studies of inquisitorial records reveal that those humanists persecuted by the Church had either followed Erasmus in his criticisms of the clergy or drifted into actual heresy. Most humanists, of course, had done neither because such matters lay outside their primary areas of interest: rhetoric, philology, and education. The Inquisition, whether Spanish or Papal, had a chilling effect on religious discourse. It did nothing, however, to attack the study of the classics, humanist taste in rhetoric and argument, or the Renaissance concept of education. Still less did it seek a return to medieval standards in the visual arts. A survey of the later sixteenth century reveals that humanist preoccupations and methods continued to flourish in the reign of Charles V and for generations to come. They did so in part because they posed no intrinsic threat to the religious revival now more commonly called the Catholic Reformation.

The great age of Renaissance as an intellectual movement had nevertheless passed before Charles retreated to his monastery. The tradition of civic humanism, important in the original creation of the movement, lost its vitality and much of its meaning when the Italian city states lost their freedom during the struggles between the Habsburgs and the Valois. Much of the old excitement over the classics died as well when there were few new classics to be discovered, edited, and publicized. The Renaissance as defined by Kristeller and his disciples was in fact self-limiting. The pioneer humanists had done their work by the 1530s. They had recovered and edited most of ancient literature, and though the tradition of scholarship they established continues in the present day, new discoveries have been rare. The Renaissance as a 're-birth' faded during the reign of Charles V, but the methods and concerns of humanism survived as did classical standards of tastes in the arts.

The Emperor's personal influence on these changes was minimal. His advisers in the early years had been strongly influenced by Erasmian humanism. Later, he supported the persecution of those who challenged the Church too openly, and to the extent that he patronized scholarship at all, favored humanists like Sepúlveda who did not wholly reject traditional modes of argument. In this he differed little from other rulers of the time. His impact on artistic patronage was also slight. He built little, and, portraits aside, was not a patron of the arts. What he did commission, however, was in the modern style.

Charles's real interest, of course, lay in politics and war to the exclusion of almost everything else. Even his interest in religion seems to have been limited to a kind of conventional layman's piety. Because he was the most powerful ruler of his day, and because the measures he undertook affected much of the known world, his impact on the events of his age should be clear and easily defined, but they are not. Just as the outlines of his character rarely emerge from the mountain of documents he created, his achievements as a statesman are hard to describe in terms broader than those approporiate to individual kingdoms and individual decisions. There is little evidence of a global vision driven by the force of a great political will. Charles V, in other words, does not conform to ideas of political leadership inspired by Napoleon or Bismarck. He was far too cautious and respectful of tradition to ride roughshod over the political structures he had inherited. Had he tried to do so in the political world of the early sixteenth century, he would almost certainly have failed. To say, therefore, as his biographer Edward Armstrong did in 1902, that 'he was not quite a good man and not quite a great man,' is probably beside the point as well as unfair. Charles V presided over wrenching changes in a way that earned the general admiration of his contemporaries. He does not bestride his age like a colossus, but his reign marks the political and religious beginning of early modern Europe.

NOTES

1 THE FORMATION OF AN EMPIRE

1. Quoted by J. Vicens Vives, 'Imperio y administración en tiempo de Carlos V,' in: *Charles Quint et son temps* (Paris, 1959), p. 12.
2. Henry J. Cohn, 'Did Bribes Induce the German Electors to Choose Charles V as Emperor in 1519?,' *German History*, vol. 19, no. 1 (2001), pp. 1–27, provides an excellent account of the electoral process while arguing that the Electors, operating on principles later expressed by Talleyrand, took the bribes and did what was best for Germany.
3. H. Angermeier, 'Reichsreform und Reformation,' *Historische Zeitschrift* 235 (1982), pp. 529–604.
4. There is an excellent discussion of Frederick's motives in: W. Borth, *Die Luthersache 1517–1524* (Lübeck, 1970), pp. 88–94.
5. James Atkinson, *The Trial of Luther* (New York, 1971), pp. 177–8.
6. R. B. Merriman, *The Rise of the Spanish Empire* (New York, 1962), III, p. 123.
7. John M. Lynch, *Spain Under the Habsburgs*, 2nd edn (New York, 1981), I, p. 52.
8. Ibid., I, pp. 74–5.

2 THE EMPIRE DEFENDED

1. R. Knecht, *Francis I* (Cambridge, 1982), p. 33. See Martyn Rady, *The Emperor Charles V* (London, 1988) p. 38 for an opposing view.
2. J. J. Scarisbrick, *Henry VIII* (Berkeley, CA, 1968), p. 206.
3. For example, see the letter of his sister, *Catherine of Portugal to Charles V*, Lisbon, 21 August, 1528 in: *Lettres des Souverains Portugais à Charles Quint et à L'imperatrice (1528–1532)* (Lisbon, 1994), pp.107–8.
4. See J. R. Hale, 'The Loss of Florentine Liberty: The Fortezza da Basso,' *Florentine Studies*, ed. N. Rubenstein (Faber, 1968), pp. 501–32.
5. F. Chabod, 'Milan o los Paises Bajos?,' *Carlos V: Homenaje de la Universidad de Granada* (Granada, 1958), pp. 331–72.
6. Charles V, *Memorias*, in: *Corpus Documental de Carlos V*, ed. M. Fernández Alvarez (Salamance, 1974–81) V, p. 91.
7. See: Thomas A. Brady, Jr., 'Phases and Strategies of the Schmalkaldic League,' *Archiv für Reformationsgeschicte* 74 (1983), pp. 162–81.

8. Karl Brandi, *The Emperor Charles V* trans. C. V. Wedgewood (London, 1939), p. 402
9. Ibid., p. 551.
10. For an account of this campaign in English, see: W. S. Maltby, *Alba* (Berkeley, CA, 1983), pp. 54–61.
11. These negotiations are described in M. Rodríguez Salgado, *The Changing Face of Empire* (Cambridge, 1988), pp. 41–3.

3 FINANCING THE EMPIRE

1. Quoted in: Henry Kamen, *Philip of Spain* (New Haven, CT, 1997), p. 31.
2. Ramón Carande, *Carlos V y sus banqueros*, 3 vols (Madrid, 1943–67), I, pp. 177, 190–2.
3. Richard Ehrenberg, *Capital and Finance in the Age of the Renaissance*, trans. H. M. Lucas (New York, 1963). Originally published, 1928.
4. James D. Tracy, *A Financial Revolution in the Habsburg Netherlands: Renten and Rentiers in the County of Holland, 1515–1565* (London, 1985), p. 90.
5. Complete schedules of *asientos* concluded during the reign of Charles V, including the names of the lenders, are found in Carande, vol. III, pp. 33f.

4 THE ORDERING OF THE EMPIRE

1. S. Haliczer, *The Comuneros of Castile* (Madison, WI, 1981), pp. 219–30.
2. A partial English translation may be found in Karl Brandi, *The Emperor Charles V*, trans. C. V. Wedgewood (London, 1939), pp. 485–9.
3. See: Helen Nader, *Liberty in Absolutist Spain: The Habsburg Sale of Towns, 1516–1700* (Baltimore, MD, 1990).
4. Antonio Calabria, *The Cost of Empire: The Finances of the Kingdom of Naples in the Time of Spanish Rule* (Cambridge, 1991), p. 132. The suggestion comes from an unpublished paper by I. A. A. Thompson.
5. See: Charles V to Juana, Regent in Spain, 25 May, 1558, quoted in: H. Kamen, *The Spanish Inquisition: A Historical Revision* (New Haven, CT, 1997), pp. 94–5.
6. This is the conservative estimate of William T. Sanders, 'The Population of the Central Mexican Symbiotic Region, the Basin of Mexico, and the Teotihuacan Valley in the Sixteenth Century,' in: William M. Denevan, ed., *The Native Population in the Americas in 1492* (Madison, WI, 1992), p. 128.
7. Benedetto Croce, *History of the Kingdom of Naples* trans. F. Frenaye (Chicago, IL, 1970), p. 135.
8. E. W. Monter, *Frontiers of Heresy* (Cambridge, 1990), p. 167.
9. See: Calabria, *The Cost of Empire*, and the essay by G. Galasso, 'Trends and Problems in Neapolitan History in the Age of Charles V,' in: *Good Government in Spanish Naples*, ed. and trans. A. Calabria and J. Marino (New York, 1990).
10. Croce, *History of the Kingdom of Naples*, p. 133.
11. G. Doria, 'Un quadrennio critico, 1575–1578,' in: E. Dini et al., eds, *Fatti e idee di storia economica nei secoli XII–XX* (Bologna, 1977), pp. 377–94.

12. This is the basic thesis of James D.Tracy, *Holland Under Habsburg Rule, 1506–1566.* (Berkeley, CA, 1990).
13. Ibid., pp. 112–13.
14. For examples, see: C. C. Hibben, *Gouda in Revolt* (Utrecht, 1983).
15. Tracy, *Holland Under Habsburg Rule*, p. 65.
16. Geoffrey Parker, *The Dutch Revolt* (London, 1977), p. 38.

5 THE SETTLEMENT OF EUROPE

1. Brandi, *The Emperor Charles V*, pp. 423–4.
2. See the comment in his Testament of 1543, ibid., p. 493.
3. This interpretation has recently been questioned by Henry Kamen, *Philip II* (New Haven, CT, 1998), p. 90. The evidence of Philip's unpopularity, however, remains convincing.
4. The first Maria was actually the younger of the two. She was the daughter of Charles's youngest sister Catherine and João III. The Maria of 1553–54 was the daughter of Charles's oldest sister Eleanor and João's father Manoel II (died 1521).
5. Charles to Ferdinand, 10 June, 1554, in: Karl Lanz, *Correspondenz des Kaiser Karls V* (Leipzig, 1848), III, p. 624.

SOURCES AND FURTHER READING

Almost any book written about the first half of the sixteenth century would provide background, at least, on the reign of Charles V. Those that have been written specifically about him, his policies, or his realms are many, but relatively few are accessible to the English-speaking reader. The golden age of Charles V scholarship began in the mid-nineteenth century and ended in the mid-twentieth. European scholars, many of them inhabitants of the Emperor's former realms, saw his reign as a defining moment in western history, even if to most of them it was a time of missed opportunities. A vast array of articles and monographs appeared in German, Italian, French, and Spanish. Most of these works are now out of print or found in journals that can be located in only the larger of research libraries. Since then, the interest of professional historians has moved away from political and institutional history, though there is still much to be learned about both. There are large gaps in our understanding of the economic history of the age as well. Religious history has been better served. A generation of solid scholarship has ensured that our understanding of the Reformation, or more accurately the reformations, of the sixteenth century is deeper and more nuanced than it was only 50 years ago. The history of war, too, has benefited from the work of those who, without ignoring the basics of weapons and strategy, have begun to examine military history in its social and economic context.

In developing these suggestions for further reading I have tried to strike a balance between scholarly importance and availability. Recent works and works in English are emphasized for obvious reasons, but it would be wrong to ignore the best contributions of an earlier age or to omit vital contributions to the literature simply because they were written in the languages of Charles V's old Empire. Many readers will command the languages needed to use them, while those who do not may nevertheless wish to gain an overall sense of the literature. This brief essay is not, however, intended to be all-inclusive. Scholars will quite properly object to the omission of this or that source, but the number of works on Charles V is vast. It would be nearly impossible, as well as inappropriate, to provide a truly comprehensive bibliography in a book intended for students and general readers.

ARCHIVES AND PRIMARY SOURCES

The correspondence and state papers of Charles V are found largely in three great archives: the Haus- Hof- und Staatsarchiv, Vienna; the Archives Générale du Royaume, Brussels; and the Archivo General de Simancas, Spain. There is a degree of overlap because copies of documents often found their way into two or more of these collections. Other letters and papers relating to the reign may be found in virtually every European archive of the period, but only some of it has been published. Samplings of Charles's correspondence may be found in K. Lanz, *Korrespondenz des Kaisers Karl V*, 3 vols (Leipzig, 1846), and M. Fernández Alvarez, *Corpus documental Carlos V*, 5 vols (Salamanca, 1974–81). Other printed documents are found in the *Collección de documentos inéditos para la historia de España*, 112 vols (Madrid, 1842–95), and in Ch. Weiss, *Papiers d'Etat du Cardinal de Granvelle*, 9 vols (Paris, 1841–52). Beginning in the nineteenth century, the British Public Record Office produced several useful series of documents, thoughtfully translated into English, that contain many documents on or about Charles V. They include: *Letters and Papers Foreign and Domestic, Henry VIII*, 21 vols (1864–1932), *Calendar of State Papers, Edward VI, Mary*, 2 vols (1861), and the indispensable *Letters, Dispatches, and State Papers relating to Negotiations between England and Spain*, 13 vols (1862–1954). Printed series of the Venetian and Papal ambassador's reports are also available, but must be used with care. Then, as now, ambassadors were often victimized by 'disinformation,' gossip, and inadequate sources.

Charles V fascinated his contemporaries, and a number of biographies were published in his own lifetme or in the generation after his death. Their quality varies widely. His own *Memorias* dictated during the summer of 1550, have been published in Spanish at the end of Fernández Alvarez, *Corpus documental*, 5 vols (Salamanca, 1974–81), and in English as *Autobiography of the Emperor Charles V*, trans. V. Simpson (London, 1862). They are as self-serving – and useful – as most autobiographies. The *Historia de Carlos V*, written by the humanist Juan Ginés de Sepúlveda, was intended as an official biography, though Charles never liked it. The modern reader will find it a panegyric that contains more rhetoric than useful fact. It has been published in the original Latin with a facing translation in Spanish (2 vols, Pozoblanco, 1995–96) and is far less useful than Alonso de Santa Cruz's, *Crónica de Carlos V*, 5 vols (Madrid, 1920–25). Other contemporary and near contemporary works in Spanish, French, Italian, and German, including those by Ulloa, des Barres, Girón, Hennicport, and Dolce, are too numerous to describe in detail and of interest primarily to specialists. An exception is the compendium produced by Fray Prudencio de Sandoval at the beginning of the seventeenth century: *Historia de la vida y hechos del emperador Carlos V*, 3 vols (Madrid, 1955–56). For those who read Spanish, Sandoval and Santa Cruz remain among the best sources on the reign.

BIOGRAPHIES AND GENERAL STUDIES

The standard modern biography of Charles V remains Karl Brandi's *The Emperor Charles V*, trans C. V. Wedgewood (London, 1939). Though a monument of historical scholarship, it emphasizes Germany at the expense of other parts of the Empire and employs a narrative style which, though eloquent, is often hard to follow. The second volume of the original German edition (2 vols, 1937–41) consists entirely of useful notes and references. R. B. Merriman, *The Rise of the Spanish*

Empire, vol. III (New York, 1925, reprinted, 1962) and M. Fernández Alvarez, *Charles V: Elected Emperor and Hereditary Ruler* (London, 1975) emphasize Spain and assume less knowledge on the part of the reader, but have little to say about Germany, the Netherlands, or Italy. Royall Tyler, *The Emperor Charles V* (London, 1956) is more even-handed geographically, but old-fashioned and rather eccentric in its judgments. It contains a useful, though not wholly accurate, chronology of the reign. The other major biography in English is the somewhat dated work by Edward Armstrong, *The Emperor Charles V*, 2 vols (London Macmillan, 1902).

All of these attempts at full-length biography suffered from the problems described in the Introduction, but they may be supplemented by a number of useful, if less ambitious, works. H. G. Koenigsberger, 'The Empire of Charles V in Europe,' *The New Cambridge Modern History*, vol. II, pp. 301–33 is a valuable essay. A good brief survey of the reign as a whole is Martyn Rady's *The Emperor Charles V* (London, 1988), a volume in the Seminar Studies in History series that includes a chronology, several documents, and a bibliography. M. J. Rodríguez-Salgado, *The Changing Face of Empire: Charles V, Philip II and Habsburg Authority, 1551–1559* (Cambridge, 1988) describes the transitional period at the end of the reign, but exaggerates the conflicts between Charles and his son, Philip II. The Emperor's last days are described in W. Stirling, *The Cloister-Life of the Emperor Charles V* (London, 1852).

A number of works appeared in 2000 to commemorate the five-hundredth anniversary of Charles's birth. Two of them deserve special mention. Arthur Kohler's *Karl V* (Munich, 2000) is a new, but rather conventional biography that is also available in Spanish. H. Soly, ed., *Charles V, 1500–1558, and His Time* (Antwerp, 2000) is a massive and beautifully illustrated collection of essays by eminent scholars, some of which are nearly book-length in themselves.

There is a substantial literature on the theories of empire espoused by Charles – or perhaps his councillors – in the early part of the reign. None of it is in English. The most useful works include P. Rassow, *Die Kaiser-Idee Karls V dargestellt an der Politik der Jahre 1528–40* (Berlin, 1932), and *Die politische Welt Karls V* (Münich, 1942); R. Menéndez Pidal, *La idea Imperial de Carlos V* (Buenos Aires, 1941) and 'Formación del fundamental pensamiento politico de Carlos V,' *Charles-Quint et son Temps* (Paris, 1959), pp. 1–8; and, above all, J. A. Maravall, 'Las etapas del pensamiento politico de Carlos V.' *Revista de estudios politicos* 100 (1958), pp. 93–146. M. Fernández Alvarez offers a broader perspective in *La politica mundial de Carlos V y Felipe II* (Madrid, 1966). On the Emperor's relationship with Gattinara, J. M. Headley, *The Emperor and his Chancellor: A Study of the Imperial Chancellery under Gattinara* (Cambridge, 1983) is authoritative. F. A. Yates, *Astraea: The Imperial Theme in the Sixteenth Century* (London, 1975), R. Strong, *Splendour at Court: Renaissance Spectacle and Illusion* (London, 1975), and J. Jacquot, ed., *Fêtes et cérémonies au temps de Charles Quint* (Paris, 1960) describe visual and ceremonial manifestations of the imperial ideal, but Peter Burke's 'Presenting and Re-presenting Charles V,' in H. Soly, *Charles V, 1500–1558*, pp. 393–477, is the best modern essay on the subject.

The best introduction to imperial finance and to the bankers and markets that supported it remains R. Ehrenberg, *Capital and Finance in the Age of the Renaissance* (London, 1928). The English translation, however, omits a chapter on Genoese banking that applies directly to the problems of Charles V. Ehrenberg should, in any case, be supplemented by works on the finances of individual realms listed below.

WAR AGAINST FRANCE AND THE OTTOMANS

Attempts to unravel the Habsburg–Valois struggles in Italy are found in most biographies of Charles V, but the detailed contemporary account in Francesco Guicciardini, *The History of Italy*, trans. S. Alexander (New York, 1969) remains indispensable. The standard biography of Francis I is R. J. Knecht, *Francis I* (Cambridge, 1982), while a brief volume in the Seminar Studies in History by the same author: *French Renaissance Monarchy: Francis I and Henry II* (London, 1984) provides a useful summary comparable to Rady's book on Charles V. F. A. Mignet, *La rivalité de Francois Ier et de Charles-Quint*, 2 vols (Paris, 1876) is still useful despite its age. Two equally venerable books on the military side of the struggle are Frederick L. Taylor, *The Art of War in Italy, 1494–1529* (Cambridge, 1921) and C. W. C. Oman, *A History of the Art of War in the Sixteenth Century* (London, 1937) which describes some of the more important battles in detail. J. Hook, *The Sack of Rome 1527* (London: Macmillan, 1972) is the standard account of that memorable disaster. A clear and useful narrative of Charles's political struggles as a whole may be found in the long essay by Geoffrey Parker, 'The Political World of Charles V,' in H. Soly, *Charles V, 1500–1558 and His Time*, pp. 113–226.

Sixteenth-century warfare and the complex military society that supported it bore little resemblance to either medieval or modern practice. J. R. Hale, *War and Society in Renaissance Europe, 1450–1620* (London, 1985) paints a vivid picture of military life in the age of Charles V, while illuminating the enormous difficulties faced by the commanders of the day. J. F. Guilmartin, *Gunpowder and Galleys: Changing Technology and Mediterranean Warfare at Sea in the Sixteenth Century* (Cambridge, 1974) provides a brilliant analysis of naval affairs with particular emphasis on galley warfare, both Muslim and Christian. Of all Charles's generals, only the Duke of Alba has received a full-length biography, though much of W. S. Maltby, *Alba* (Berkeley, CA, 1983) emphasizes the Duke's political activities, and more than half of it deals with the reign of Philip II.

The Ottoman Empire has received far less attention from western historians than it deserves, but Halil Inalcik, *The Ottoman Empire: The Classical Age, 1300–1600* (New York, 1973) provides an introduction to this enormous topic. There are in addition several books on North Africa in French and English. Those in English include J. M. Abun-Nasr, *A History of the Maghrib* (Cambridge, 1975), and Andrew Hess, *The Forgotten Frontier: A History of the Sixteenth-Century Ibero-African Frontier* (Chicago, IL, 1978). C. M. Kortepeter, *Ottoman Imperialism during the Reformation: Europe and the Caucasus* (New York, 1972) provides a broad perspective in relatively few pages.

THE NETHERLANDS

The reign of Charles V in the Netherlands has received far less attention than either the age of the Revolt or the glories of his Burgundian predecessors. Much of what has been written is in Dutch and is therefore inaccessible to most English readers. The best place to begin is with an understanding of the society itself. Richard Vaughn's *Valois Burgundy* (London, 1975) provides an excellent introduction, while his *Charles the Bold* (London, 1973) describes the origins of many of the problems inherited by Charles V. Economic developments in the Low Countries are analyzed in J. de Vries, *The Dutch Rural Economy in the Golden Age, 1500–1700* (New Haven, CT, 1974), and in the statistics-laden work by H. van der Wee, *The Growth of the Antwerp Market and the European Economy*, 3 vols (The Hague, 1963). Each of Charles's regents has been the subject of a biography by J. de Iongh: *Margaret of Austria: Regent of the Netherlands* (London, 1954) and *Mary of Hungary: Second Regent of the Netherlands* (London, 1959). *Mary* is much the better book, though both suffer from a popularizing style and minimal documentation.

Two indispensable studies on fiscal and institutional development whose implications transcend the province of Holland are James D. Tracy, *A Financial Revolution in the Habsburg Netherlands:'Renten' and 'Renteniers' in the County of Holland, 1515–1566* (Berkeley, CA, 1985), and *Holland under Habsburg Rule, 1506–1566* (Berkeley, CA, 1990). P. Rosenfeld, 'The Provincial Governors of the Netherlands from the Minority of Charles V to the Revolt,' *Government in Reformation Europe 1520–60*, ed. H. J. Cohn (New York, 1971), pp. 257–64 is a brief but informative article. Religious issues are discussed in Phyllis Mack Crew, *Calvinist Preaching and Iconoclasm in the Netherlands, 1544–1569* (Cambridge, 1978), and C. Krahn, *Dutch Anabaptism* (The Hague, 1968). A. Duke, 'Salvation by Coercion: The Controversy surrounding the Inquisition in the Low Countries on the Eve of the Revolt,' *Reformation Principle and Practice, Essays in Honour of A. G. Dickens*, ed. P. Brooks (London, 1980), pp. 135–56 provides a good summary of the government's policies and the reactions they provoked. Some of the conclusions set forth by James D. Tracy in 'Heresy Law and Centralization under Mary of Hungary,' *Archiv für Reformationsgeschicte*, 73 (1982), pp. 284–308 may also be found in his *Holland under Habsburg Rule*.

Charles V may not have been directly responsible for the Revolt of the Netherlands, but no discussion of his reign is possible without considering the cataclysm that occurred under his son, Philip II. Geoffrey Parker, *The Dutch Revolt* (Ithaca, NY, 1977) is a more detailed account that supercedes Peter Geyl, *The Revolt of the Netherlands* 2nd edn (London, 1958). Both, however, are useful, and both provide insights into the problems of the preceeding era.

SPAIN AND AMERICA

Two general studies of Spain under the Habsburgs are indispensable: J. H. Elliott, *Imperial Spain, 1469–1716* (New York, 1963), and John Lynch, *Spain under the Habsburgs* 2nd edn, 2 vols (New York, 1981). A somewhat revisionist view is proposed by H. Kamen, *Spain 1469–1714: A Society of Conflict* (London, 1983). All three, of course, go far beyond the reign of Charles V. P. Chaunu, *L'Espagne de Charles-Quint* is especially useful on social and economic matters. J. N. Hilgarth, *The Spanish Kingdoms 1250–1516*, vol. 2 (Oxford, 1978) is the best overall source of information on the fifteenth-century background, while Peggy Liss, *Isabel the Queen* (Oxford, 1992) offers a sympathetic biography of Charles's grandmother.

The *comunero* revolt has been the subject of several books, the best of which is Stephen Haliczer, *The Comuneros of Castile: The Forging of a Revolution, 1475–1521* (Madison, WI, 1981). Haliczer also provides a useful sketch of the reform policies undertaken by Charles in the wake of the revolt. J. Pérez, *La révolution des 'Comunidades' de Castille (1520–1521)* (Bordeaux, 1970, Spanish edn, Madrid, 1977) offers a somewhat different perspective. Spanish administration in this period has otherwise been badly served. Both Elliott and Lynch provide brief descriptions, but most monographs on the subject emphasize the reign of Philip II. J. A. Escudero, *Los secretarios de Estado y del despacho, 1474–1724*, 4 vols (Madrid, 1964) describes the evolution of the secretarial office and Ernst Schäfer, *El consejo real y supremo de las indias*, 2 vols (Seville, 1935–47) provides the only systematic study of a council to date. There is, however, a biography of Francisco de los Cobos in English: Hayward Keniston, *Francisco de los Cobos* (Pittsburgh, PA, 1960). Unfortunately, Keniston was a specialist in Spanish literature and his book empasizes the personal at the expense of the political. R. Carande, *Carlos V y sus banqueros*, 3 vols (Madrid, 1943–67) is fundamental to an understanding of the realm's finances. The alienation of lands and its effect on Spanish political development is described in Helen Nader, *Liberty in Habsburg Spain: The Habsburg Sale of Towns, 1516–1700* (Baltimore, MD, 1993).

Much of the work on Spanish intellectual life in the reign of Charles V has concentrated on Erasmian humanism and its somewhat problematic relationship with the *alumbrados* and Protestantism. The standard book on the subject remains Marcel Bataillon's *Erasme et l'Espagne* ((Paris, 1937). There is a revised and expanded edition in Spanish. 2 vols, Mexico, 1950). LuAnn Homza, *Religious Authority in the Spanish Renaissance* (Baltimore, MD, 2000) provides new perspectives on many of these same issues. The best work on the *alumbrados* remains Antonio Márquez, *Los alumbrados: origenes y filosophía (1525–1559)*, 2nd edn (Madrid, 1980). Gordon Kinder, 'Spain', in: *The Early Reformation in Europe*, ed. A. Pettegree (Cambridge, 1992), pp. 215–37 is a good brief survey of Spanish Protestantism, while José Nieto, *Juan de Valdés and the Origins of the Spanish and Italian Reformations* (Geneva, 1970) deals with an official of the Emperor who was involved in all three movements. Of the many books on the Spanish Inquisition: the most useful is a general survey by Henry Kamen, *The Spanish Inquisition: A Historical Revision* (New Haven, CT, 1997). It may or may not be the author's final word on a subject that he has treated in two earlier volumes. Kamen emphasizes Castile; William Monter, *Frontiers of Heresy: The Spanish Inquisition from the Basque Lands to Sicily* (Cambridge, 1990) is excellent for the other Spanish kingdoms. The flowering of political thought under Charles V is described by J. A. Fernández Santamaria in *The State, War, and Peace: Spanish Political Thought in the Renaissance 1516–1559* (Cambridge, 1977), a book which also casts a somewhat different light on Spanish scholarship as a whole. Charles V preceded the golden age of Spanish art, but Jonathan Brown, *Painting in Spain, 1500–1700* (New Haven, CT, 1998) contains a useful chapter on art and patronage during his reign.

The literature on Spain in the Americas is too vast to permit more than a sampling here. J. H. Elliott, *The Old World and the New, 1492–1650* (Cambridge, 1970) is a good interpretative essay. There are many works on the conquests of Mexico and Peru, but it would be hard to imagine for Mexico an improvement over Bernal Díaz del Castillo's contemporary masterpiece *The Conquest of New Spain*, trans.

J. M. Cohen (Penguin, 1965). The seminal study on the biological and cultural consequences of the conquests is Alfred W. Crosby, *The Columbian Exchange* (Westport, CT, 1972). C. H. Haring, *The Spanish Empire in America* (New York, 1947) remains the best survey of Spanish administration, while Lewis Hanke, *The Spanish Struggle for Justice in the Conquest of America* (Philadelphia, PA, 1949), best summarizes the author's lifetime of work on Las Casas, the debate over the Indians, and the introduction of the New Laws.

ITALY

Italy in the sixteenth century was probably too complex to be described in a useful general history. None has been written, but Guicciardini's contemporary *History of Italy* provides useful information on many of the states and their rulers in the first half of the Emperor's reign. There are also a number of works on Charles's dominions. The standard histories of Naples are Benedetto Croce's *History of the Kingdom of Naples*, trans. F. Frenaye (Chicago, IL, 1970), still useful in spite of its philosophical preoccupations, and G. Coniglio, *Il regno di Napoli al tiempo de Carlo V* (Naples, 1934). The kingdom's finances are discussed in A. Calabria, *The Cost of Empire: The Finances of the Kingdom of Naples in the Time of Spanish Rule* (Cambridge, 1991). The volume edited by A. Calabria and J. Marino, *Good Government in Spanish Naples* (New York, 1990) contains a number of useful essays, including G. Galasso's 'Trends and Problems in Neapolitan History in the Age of Charles V,' pp. 13–78. Sicily is less well served. Mack Smith, *A History of Sicily*, vol. I (London, 1968) is too broad to provide much more than an introduction to the kingdom's history under Charles V, and there are two works by H. G. Koenigsberger, 'The Parliament of Sicily and the Spanish Empire,' in his *Estates and Revolutions* (Ithaca, NY, 1971), pp. 80–93, and *The Government of Sicily under Philip II*, first pub. 1951, reprinted as *The Practice of Empire* (Ithaca, NY, 1969). Both help to provide context. There has been nothing in English on Milan since C. M. Ady's *A History of Milan under the Sforza* (London, 1907), which ends in 1535. The standard history is Federico Chabod, *Lo stato di Milano nell' impero di Carlo V* (Rome, 1934), republished with some of the author's other studies as *Lo stato e la vita religiosa a Milano nell'epoca di Carlo V* (Turin, 1971).

For Charles's dealings with the papacy there is still no substitute for L. von Pastor, *The History of the Popes*, trans. R. Kerr, vols 9–13 (London, 1950), but J. Hook, 'Clement VII, the Colonna and Charles V,' *European Studies Review* 2 (1972), pp. 281–99 provides a glimpse of the Emperor's manipulation of vassals within the Papal States. On Protestantism in Italy and the efforts of the Papal Inquisition to control it, there is S. Caponetto, *The Protestant Reformation in Sixteenth-Century Italy*, trans. J. and A. Tedeschi (Kirksville, MO, 1999), a comprehensive, if controversial, treatment of its subject.

GERMANY AND CENTRAL EUROPE

The problems of sixteenth-century Germany can seem almost impenetrable, especially to those who do not read German For them, the best place to begin is with one of the many excellent surveys of the Reformation that have been published on a regular basis in both England and America. Biographies of Luther are nearly as common. A complete listing is not appropriate here, but R. H. Bainton, *Here I Stand: A Life of Martin Luther* (New York, 1951) or J. Kittelson, *Luther the Reformer* (Minneapolis, MN, 1988) are good introductions to his complex and controversial life. For those who do read German, there are two good recent interpretations of German history in the sixteenth century: Heinz Schilling, *Aufbruch und Krise: Deutschland, 1517–1648* (Berlin, 1988), and Horst Rabe, *Deutsche Geshicte 1500–1600* (Munich, 1991).

No single work has done full justice to the complexity of the Empire and its institutions, but an essay by H. Gross, 'The Holy Roman Empire in Early Modern Times: Constitutional Reality and Legal Theory,' in: *The Old Reich: Essays on German Political Institutions, 1493–1806*, ed. J. A. Vann and S. W. Rowan (Brussels, 1974), pp. 1–29 is helpful, as is a reference book, *The Holy Roman Empire: A Dictionary Handbook*, ed. J. Zophy (Westport, CT, 1980). Volker Press, *Das Reichskammergericht in der deutschen Geschicte* (Wetzlar, 1987) examines the role of this important institution as it developed over time. An older work, F. L. Carsten, *Princes and Parliaments in Germany from the Fifteenth to the Eighteenth Century* (Oxford, 1959) surveys the development of representative institutions, but for those seeking detailed information on individual states a broad range of monographs and local histories is available.

The most striking events of the reign in Germany have been the subject of many books and articles. The revolutions of the 1520s are covered in W. R. Hitchcock, *The Background of the Knight's Revolt, 1522–23* (Berkeley, CA, 1958) and P. Blickle, *The Revolution of 1525*, trans. T. A. Brady and H. C. E. Midelfort (Baltimore, MD, 1981). Blickle has largely superceded Günther Franz, *Die deutsche Bauernkrieg* (München and Berlin, 1933). P. S. Fichtner, *Ferdinand I of Austria,1503–1564* (Boulder, CO, 1982) is essential to an understanding of Charles's brother and the role he played in Germany and Eastern Europe. The critical first years of Ferdinand's reign are described by A. Lhotsky, *Das Zeitalter des Hauses Österreich. Die ersten Jahre der Regierung Ferdinands I, 1520–27* (Cologne and Vienna, 1971).

The politics of the 1530 Diet of Augsburg are described in G. Krodel, 'Law, Order, and the Almighty Taler: The Empire in Action at the 1530 Diet of Augsburg,' *Sixteenth Century Journal*, 12 (1982), pp.75–106 and in the older but still useful E. M. Mayer, 'Forschungen zur Politik Karls V während des augsburger Reichstags von 1530,' *Archiv für Reformationsgeschichte* 13 (1916), pp. 40–73, 124–46. On Charles's religious policies at this time, see: W. Reinhard, 'Die kirchenpolitischen Vorstellungen Kaiser Karls V, ihr Grundlagen und ihr Wandel,' *Confessio Augustana und Confutatio. Der Augsburger Reichstag 1530 und die Einheit der Kirche*, ed. E. Iserloh (Münster, 1980), pp. 62–100.

The shifting course of papal–imperial diplomacy on the question of a Church council must be traced in the pages of Charles's biographies and in Pastor's *History of the Popes*. The meetings at Regensburg are covered in Basil Hall, 'The Colloquies between Catholics and Protestants, 1539–1541,' *Studies in Church History* 7 (1971), pp. 235–66. P. Matheson, *Cardinal Contarini at Regensburg* (Oxford, 1972), and Elisabeth Gleason, *Gasparo Contarini: Venice, Rome, and Reform* (Berkeley, CA, 1993) are studies of the reforming Cardinal who sought a reconcilliation with the Protestants. When Paul III at last decided to call the Council of Trent, its deliberations set the Church's course for generations to come. H. Jedin, *A History of the Council of Trent*, 3 vols, trans. E. Graf (Edinburgh, 1962) is the classic treatment of its subject.

On the Schmalkaldic wars, their causes and their aftermath, Fritz Hartung's brief essay, *Karl V und die deutschen Reichstände von 1546–1555* (Darmstadt, 1971, first pub. Halle, 1910) remains useful. T. A. Brady, *Turning Swiss: Cities and Empires, 1450–1550* (Cambridge, 1985) describes the complex relationship between towns and principalities and provides valuable insights into the workings of the Schmalkaldic League. The same author's 'Phases and Strategies of the Schmalkaldic League: A Perspective after 450 Years,' *Archiv für Reformationsgeschichte* 74 (1983), pp. 162–86 is a good short survey. H. Petri has written two useful articles on the complex situation in northwest Germany that helped to provoke the Schmalkaldic wars: 'Nordwestdeutschland im Wechselspiegel der Politik Karls V und Philipps der Grossmütigen von Hessen,' *Zeitschrift des Vereins für hessische Landesgeschicte und Landeskunde* 71 (1960), pp. 37–60, and 'Herzog Heinrich der Jungere von Braunschweig-Wolfenbüttel,' *Archiv für Reformationsgeschichte* 72 (1981), pp. 122–58. The military aspects of the wars may be studied in A. Schüz, *Der Donaufeldzug Karls V im Jahre 1546* (Tübingen, 1930), or, more briefly and in English, in W. S. Maltby's *Alba* (Berkeley, CA, 1983).

Anger over the Augsburg Interim helped to provoke the next great crisis in German affairs: the princes' attack on Charles in 1552. H. Rabe, *Reichsbund und Interim* (Cologne and Vienna, 1971) is a detailed study of the 1548 Diet of Augsburg and its aftermath. The Emperor's scheme for imperial reform is analyzed by M. Salomies, *Die Pläne Kaiser Karls V für eine Reichsreform mit Hilfe eines allgemeinen Bundes* (Helsinki, 1953). The best source on the debâcle of 1552 is probably H. Lutz, *Christianitas afflicta: Europa, das Reich und die päpstliche Politik im Niedergang der Hegemonie Kaiser Karls V* (Göttingen, 1964). Maurice of Saxony could be the subject of a popular novel. Until then, we have the short, scholarly biography by Karlheinz Blaschke, *Moritz von Sachsen* (Göttingen, 1984). His role in the revolt against Charles may be examined in K. E. Born, 'Moritz von Sachsen und die Fürstenverschwörung gegen Karl V,' *Historische Zeitschrift* 191 (1960), pp. 18–66. The relevant documents on Maurice's career to 1548 may be found in *Politische Korrespondenz des Herzogs und Kurfürsten Moritz von Sachsen*, ed. J. Herrmann and G. Wartenberg (Berlin, 1978).

The temporary resolution of these conflicts by the Peace of Augsburg in 1555 and the consequences of that peace for the subsequent development of Germany became in later years a major source of controversy. Two articles in English on the Peace itself are: Lewis W. Spitz, 'Particularism and Peace, Ausgburg 1555,' *Church History* 25 (1956), pp. 110–26, and the interpretive essay by H. Tüchle, 'The Peace of Augsburg: New Order or Lull in the Fighting,' in: H. J. Cohn, ed., *Government in Reformation Europe* (London, 1971), pp. 145–65. Opinions on the aftermath of the Peace vary. An older school of historians believed that Augsburg perpetuated the fragmentation of the Empire and inhibited the 'natural' development of the German state. A more modern view, typified by Gerald Strauss, 'The Holy Roman Empire Revisited,' *Central European History* 11 (1978), pp. 290–301, is more positive. Thomas A. Brady, Jr. has offered useful reflections on this issue in several articles. They have been collected, along with some of his other essays on the Empire, in *Communities, Politics, and Reformation in Early Modern Europe* (Leiden, 1998). The related subject of Charles V and his place in German history is discussed at length in Chapter Six of this book.

CHRONOLOGY

1500	Charles is born at Ghent
1504	Death of Isabella of Castile
1506	Death of Charles's father, Philip 'the Handsome'
1515	Charles is proclaimed ruler of the Netherlands
1516	Death of Ferdinand of Aragon Charles is proclaimed King of Castile and Aragon
1517	Charles lands in Spain for the first time Luther posts his 95 Theses at Wittenberg
1519	Death of Emperor Maximilian I Occupation of Württemberg by the Swabian League Charles is elected Emperor
1519–21	Conquest of Mexico by Hernán Cortés
1519–22	Circumnavigation of the globe by Magellan and Sebastian del Cano *Germanías* revolts in Valencia
1520	Charles leaves Spain for Germany Outbreak of the *comunero* revolt in Castile
1521	Diet of Worms; condemnation of Luther Death of Chancellor Guillaume de Croy, Lord of Chièvres Outbreak of the first war with France Capture and annexation of Tournai by Charles's forces Defeat of the *comuneros* at Villalar Unsuccessful French invasion of Navarre Imperial army captures Milan Publication of the first *placards* against heresy in the Netherlands
1522	Election of Pope Adrian VI French defeated at Battle of La Bicocca Charles promises Austrian lands and the Imperial succession to Ferdinand Treaty of Windsor with Henry VIII of England Charles returns to Spain

1523	Revolt of the Imperial Knights in Germany The Duke of Bourbon defects to Charles Election of Pope Clement V
1523–24	Annexation of Frisia
1524–26	Great Peasants' War in Germany
1525	Battle of Pavia; capture of Francis I by imperial forces
1526	Treaty of Madrid Charles marries Isabella of Portugal Formation of the League of Cognac against Charles First Diet of Speyer Battle of Mohács Ferdinand elected King of Bohemia
1527	Sack of Rome Henry VIII petitions for divorce from Catherine of Aragon Birth of Prince Philip (later Philip II of Spain) French invade Milan and besiege Naples War with Gelre; annexation of Utrecht and Overijssel Ferdinand occupies Croatia, Slovenia, and western Hungary
1528	Andrea Doria defects to Charles French abandon the siege of Naples
1529	French defeated at the Battle of Landriano Second Diet of Speyer: the 'Protestestation' of Speyer First Ottoman siege of Vienna Peace of Cambrai ('The Ladies' Peace') Marburg Colloquy
1530	Charles crowned Emperor by Clement VII at Bologna Restoration of the Medici at Florence Restoration of Francesco Maria Sforza at Milan Death of Grand Chancellor Mercurino de Gattinara Diet of Augsburg Augsburg Confession Death of Margaret of Burgundy, Regent of the Netherlands
1531	Mary of Hungary appointed Regent of the Netherlands Election of Ferdinand as King of the Romans Formation of the Schmalkaldic League
1531–32	Conquest of Peru
1532	Ottoman retreat from Vienna
1533	Restoration of Württemberg to Duke Ulrich
1534	Election of Pope Paul III
1535	Conquest of Tunis Death of Francesco Maria Sforza; Milan reverts to the Empire

1536   War with France; failure of Charles's campaign in Provence
          War with Gelre; annexation of Groningen, Drenthe, and the
          Ommelanden
          Reorganization of the Spanish army: formation of the *tercios*

1537   Truce with France signed at Bomy

1538   Formation of the Catholic League in the Empire
          Meeting of Charles and Francis at Aigues Mortes
          Failure of the *Sisa* on food in Castile
          Naval battle of Prevesa

1539   Death of the Empress Isabella
          Charles journeys to the Netherlands through France

1540   Charles suppresses rebellion at Ghent

1541   Diet and Colloquy of Regensberg
          Failure of the expedition against Algiers

1542   Resumption of war with France: Turkish fleet winters at Toulon
          William of Cleves invades the Netherlands
          Defeat of Henry of Brunswick by the Schmalkaldic League
          Publication of the 'New Laws' in the Indies
          Re-establishment of the Papal Inquisition

1543   Charles defeats William of Cleves, annexes Gelre
          Annexation of Cambrai

1544   Battle of Ceresole
          Peace of Crépy

1545   Beginning of the Council of Trent

1546   Conversion of Frederick of the Palatinate
          Second Diet of Regensburg
          Beginning of the Schmalkaldic War: campaign on the
          upper Danube
          Death of Henry VIII of England

1547   Death of Francis I of France; accession of Henry II
          Battle of Mühlberg, defeat of John Frederick of Saxony
          Imprisonment of John Frederick and Philip of Hesse
          Tripartite Division of Hungary

1547–48   Diet of Augsburg; proclamation of the Augsburg Interim

1548   Separation of the Netherlands from the Empire

1551   Succession pact among the Habsburgs

1552   Revolt of the German princes: Charles flees to Innsbruck
          Henry II captures Metz, Toul, and Verdun
          Peace of Passau

1552–53   Siege of Metz by Charles fails

1553–54   New invasions of the Netherlands by Henry II

1554   Charles abdicates the Kingdom of Naples in favor of Philip
          Philip marries Mary of England
          Fall of Siena

1555   Peace of Augsburg
          Philip renounces his claim as King of the Romans

1555–56   Charles abdicates as King of Spain and ruler of the Netherlands

1556–57   War between Philip II and Pope Paul IV

1557   Charles retires to Yuste
          Philip II suspends payments on the Castilian debt
          French defeat at the battle of St Quentin

1558   Death of Charles
          Death of Mary of Hungary
          Death of Mary of England

1559   Treaty of Câteau-Cambrésis; end of the Habsburg–Valois wars

GENEALOGICAL CHART

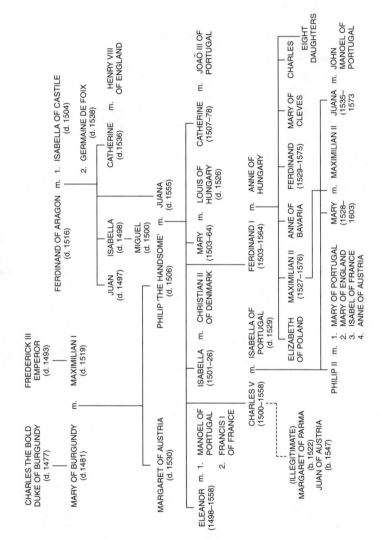

INDEX

147

DATE DUE
